Making Meaning, Making Change

Participatory Curriculum Development
for Adult ESL Literacy

Making Meaning, Making Change

Participatory Curriculum Development
for Adult ESL Literacy

Elsa Roberts Auerbach

A publication of the Center for Applied Linguistics
prepared by the National Clearinghouse on Literacy Education,
an adjunct ERIC Clearinghouse

Language in Education

Theory & Practice

ERIC

CAL

Language in Education: Theory and Practice 78

This publication was prepared with funding from the Office of Educational Research and Improvement, U.S. Department of Education, under contract No. RI 89166001. The opinions expressed in this publication do not necessarily reflect the positions or policies of OERI or ED.

Editorial/production supervision: Fran Keenan
Interior design: Julie Booth
Cover design: Vincent Sagart

Printed in the United States of America

10 9 8 7 6 5 4 3 2 1

ISBN 0-93-735479-1

Language in Education: Theory and Practice

ERIC (Educational Resources Information Center) is a nationwide network of information centers, each responsible for a given educational level or field of study. ERIC is supported by the Office of Educational Research and Improvement of the U.S. Department of Education. The basic objective of ERIC is to make current developments in educational research, instruction, and personnel preparation readily accessible to educators and members of related professions.

The ERIC Clearinghouse on Languages and Linguistics (ERIC/CLL), one of the specialized clearinghouses in the ERIC system, is operated by the Center for Applied Linguistics (CAL). ERIC/CLL is specifically responsible for the collection and dissemination of information on research in languages and linguistics and on the application of research to language teaching and learning.

ERIC/CLL commissions recognized authorities in languages and linguistics to write about current issues in the field. The resultant monographs, intended for use by educators, researchers, and others interested in language education, are published under the series title, *Language in Education: Theory and Practice*. The series includes practical guides for classroom teachers, state-of-the-art papers, research reviews, and collected reports.

For further information on the ERIC system and ERIC/CLL, write to the ERIC Clearinghouse on Languages and Linguistics, Center for Applied Linguistics, 1118 22nd Street, NW, Washington, DC 20037.

Vickie Lewelling
ERIC/CLL Publications Coordinator

National Clearinghouse on Literacy Education
An Adjunct ERIC Clearinghouse

In September 1989, the Center for Applied Linguistics (CAL) was awarded a contract to expand the activities of the ERIC Clearinghouse on Languages and Linguistics (ERIC/CLL) through the establishment of an Adjunct ERIC Clearinghouse, the National Clearinghouse on Literacy Education (NCLE). The specific focus of NCLE is literacy education for limited-English proficient adults and out-of-school youth.

The creation of NCLE has enabled ERIC/CLL to expand the *Language in Education: Theory and Practice* series to include monographs targeted specifically to literacy educators working with language minority adults and youth. The purpose of the monographs is to help practitioners assist these individuals to achieve full literacy in English and, whenever possible, in their native language.

Monographs commissioned by NCLE are written by recognized authorities in adult literacy education and ESL (English as a second language). They are edited and prepared for publication by NCLE staff members. The editing and production of *Making Meaning, Making Change: Participatory Curriculum Development for Adult ESL Literacy* were coordinated by Fran Keenan.

For further information on NCLE publications and services, contact the National Clearinghouse on Literacy Education, Center for Applied Linguistics, 1118 22nd Street, NW, Washington, DC 20037.

Fran Keenan and Joy Kreeft Peyton, NCLE Publications Coordinators

Contents

Acknowledgements

Ann Cason, Rosario Gomez-Sanford, Loren McGrail, Andrea Nash, and Madeline Rhum deserve the real credit for this book because it is their work on which it is based; their creativity and commitment as teachers speak for themselves throughout the book.

Much of the work reported here took place in the context of the University of Massachusetts (UMass) English Family Literacy Project, a collaboration between the UMass-Boston Bilingual/ESL Graduate Studies Program and the following centers: the Community Learning Center in Cambridge, MA; *El Centro del Cardenal* (The Cardinal Cushing Center for the Spanish-Speaking) in Boston; and the Jackson-Mann Community School in Allston-Brighton, MA.

I would like to express my deepest appreciation to the staff of those centers for welcoming the project and for helping to guide it. Special gratitude goes to the students whose work appears in this book and to all the others who taught us about their ways of learning and teaching. I also want to thank Candace Mitchell, Cathie Wallace, the staff of the Cambridge Oral History Center, our co-workers in the Boston adult literacy community, and the many others who shared their experience in workshops and training sessions. Further, I would like to express gratitude to Donaldo Macedo, Director of the UMass Bilingual/ESL Graduate Studies Program, for making this project possible through his many efforts on its behalf and his constant support. Nina Wallerstein, Gail Weinstein-Shr, Janet Isserlis, and an anonymous reader provided invaluable criticism of the original version of *Making Meaning, Making Change*, as well as suggestions for revision. I would also like to thank Fran Keenan for her many hours of hard work making meaning and making changes in the process of transforming the manuscript into a book. Finally, Barbara Graceffa deserves special acknowledgement for her unending and cheerful attention to all the details of making the Family Literacy Project a reality from the moment it was conceived to its final stages.

Much of the work reported on in this book was funded by Title VII, Office of Bilingual Education and Minority Language Affairs (OBEMLA), grant number G008635277, procurement number 003JH60021. The views, opinions, and findings contained in this book are not to be construed as OBEMLA's position or policy, unless so designated.

Introduction

What This Book Is... and What It Is Not

This is a book that looks backward and looks forward; it is written both as a retroactive documentation of one participatory adult ESL literacy project (the University of Massachusetts (UMass) Family Literacy Project) and as a guide for others undertaking similar projects. If there's one thing that we learned during the course of our work, it's that every group of students is different; what happens with any given class depends on who the participants are, what their concerns are, and the contexts of their lives. Each group brings its own set of family situations, language and literacy backgrounds, community problems, employment circumstances, and cultural strengths to the learning situation, and each of these factors must be taken into account in curriculum development. The most effective curricula are those tailored to and developed with participating learners. The key in a participatory approach is centering instruction on the real (rather than imagined) issues of each group; the only way to do this is through collaborative investigation and decision-making.

It is for this reason that we have written a curriculum guide rather than a curriculum: We don't believe that a single generic, prepackaged sequence of themes, language items, or activities can possibly fit all sets of circumstances or students. Instead of trying to *cover* content that has been predetermined, teachers need to *discover* content that's important to their own students. To do this, they need a conceptual framework, a set of procedures for creating context-specific curricula emerging out of particular conditions, and concrete examples of the process in practice.

In accordance with this perspective, *Making Meaning, Making Change* is intended as a *description* rather than a *prescription:* We aren't trying to tell anyone what to do or what content to cover tomorrow. Rather we are describing what we did, why we did it, and how others can follow similar processes to discover what's relevant for their students and to involve them in building curriculum around this relevant material. Thus, unlike traditional curriculum guides which specify the structure, sequence, and content for instruction, this book raises issues about teaching and curriculum development, inviting readers to share experiences, make their assumptions about literacy explicit, and work together in investigating alternatives. The form of the book itself is interactive, challenging the readers as teachers, researchers, and administrators to use it as a framework for questioning beliefs, reexamining taken-for-granted assumptions and guiding inquiry in regard to practice.

Our Context: The UMass Family Literacy Project

Since the central tenet of a participatory approach is that curricula must emerge from and be responsive to the particular context of each group of participants, it is important to start by describing our own context in undertaking this project. The UMass Family Literacy Project was one of many projects funded by the U.S. Department of Education's Office of Bilingual Education and Minority Language Affairs (OBEMLA) through Title VII, the Bilingal Education Act, for the purpose of providing English literacy instruction to the parents of children in bilingual education programs. Our project was a collaboration between the Bilingual/ESL Graduate Studies Program at UMass/Boston and three Boston area community-based adult literacy centers: the Jackson-Mann Community School, The Cardinal Cushing Center for the Spanish-Speaking/El Centro del Cardenal, and the Community Learning Center.

Each of the sites is a well-established literacy center with deep, long-standing ties to the community where it is located; the family literacy work was thus an additional component to ongoing programs, sharing certain features of these programs but differing in other ways. We worked primarily with adults, serving a total of approximately 150 students per year. Students came from many language groups (up to 26 at one time); only one site, the Cardinal Cushing Center, serves a single language group (Spanish speakers).

Staff of the project at any given time included three full-time teachers, a half-time curriculum specialist, and a coordinator. Ann Cason, Rosario (Charo) Gomez-Sanford, Loren McGrail, and Madeline Rhum were the teachers, (Charo replaced Loren at the end of the second year); Andy Nash was the curriculum specialist (in addition to teaching half-time through other funding), and Elsa Auerbach was the coordinator. All of us are women, three are mothers, four speak English as a first language, and one (Charo) is a Bolivian who speaks Quechua as her first language, Spanish as her second, and English as her fifth! While we had different job titles, we tried to function in a participatory way with each other, sharing decision-making, curriculum development, classroom concerns, and dissemination tasks. None of this was without struggle: We had to work at redefining roles and relationships along the way in our attempt to "practice what we preach."

Behind every sentence of this introduction, there's a story. The fact that the project was a university-community collaboration, that it was tied to but separate from existing programs, that students spoke many languages, that teachers were similar in some ways but different in others—all of these aspects of our own context shaped the direction of our project and the issues we had to address along the way. I'll save the stories for later, but it's important to note that our work, like work with students, was the result of a particular set of choices and conditions.

The one aspect of our context that is important to explore at this point is that our project was funded as a family literacy project. From the outset, this presented us with particular issues and questions: Should we work with parents and children together? Should we link the project with the public school system? Should we focus exclusively on content relating to parenting? What if issues arose in class that seemed unrelated to family literacy as it is traditionally defined—issues such as work or housing or immigration? Did they still count as family literacy work?

As we struggled to implement our approach, we realized that while many of these issues were particular to our project, the general approach that we were developing applied equally to any adult literacy program; that is to say, effective programs must always take into account the social context of participants' lives, including family situations, concerns about children, work, and whatever else arises from the conditions of students' lives. Moreover, we realized that any participatory approach will, by definition, have its own set of issues—a workplace program will have to deal with questions about whose agenda to follow, how to deal with conflicts between workers' and management's needs, and so on—and that this particularity *is* precisely what is *common to curricula that start with participants' lived experience.*

Similar issues arose in conceptualizing this book: Should the book be framed as a guide to developing family literacy programs or more broadly as a guide to participatory curriculum development for any adult ESL/literacy program? The original version of this book, published by UMass, started with a chapter explaining the rationale for applying a participatory approach to family literacy, namely that family literacy development depends in large part on the extent to which literacy is socially significant in family life, and as such, family literacy programs must focus on using literacy as a tool to deal with concerns that arise from participants' daily reality. The remainder of the original guide elaborated a model and tools for finding out and developing curricula around participants' issues, whatever they may be. Thus, its relevance went beyond family literacy programs. In preparing this version of the book for a broader audience, its focus has been revised to reflect this duality: It describes a general approach for building curricula out of specific contexts and uses the particular experiences of one project (in this case a family literacy project) to illustrate its implementation.

How This Book Was Written

Although our goal in the UMass Family Literacy Project was to be fully participatory in all aspects of our work, we often divided tasks according to differing roles. An example of this is the way that this book came to be written. As we discussed producing our final report, a variety of perspectives emerged on what it should look like. The teachers felt strongly about maintaining an independent voice to represent their experiences in the classroom; they wanted to ensure that accounts of practice were presented from practitioners' perspective. Thus, they formed their own writing group, producing *Talking Shop: A Curriculum Sourcebook for Participatory Adult ESL*, a collection of "windows on the classroom" (Nash, Cason, Gomez-Sanford, McGrail & Rhum, in press). At the same time, however, we felt a need for a different kind of piece that would generalize from our collective experience, weaving it together into an overview of the curriculum development process as a whole; this ultimately was to become *Making Meaning, Making Change*.

Thus, we ended up with two volumes—companion pieces—each representing a different focus and a different perspective. Where one analyzes theoretical and methodological aspects of the components of curriculum development, the other focuses on particular accounts of curriculum cycles as they played themselves out in the classroom. Where *Making Meaning, Making Change* is written primarily from the perspective of the project coordinator, *Talking Shop* is written fully from the teachers' perspective.

In each case, we started with group discussions of content, format, and organization; however, the teachers' writing was much more collaborative in the revising stages. They met regularly to share drafts and give feedback; in the early stages, I got feedback to the extent teachers had the time to provide it, but as the funding ran out, the process became increasingly individual. Although the process was relatively individual, the content comes from extensive documentation of group work collected throughout the project: minutes of meetings and workshops, teaching materials, examples of student work, and teachers' journals. Thus, the "we" in this guide means different things at different points: Sometimes it reflects direct reporting of group discussions, paraphrasing or quoting teachers as they share insights and experiences; at other times, it represents the coordinator's interpretation/extension of analyses reached through a group process.

Our Audience

One of the first questions we grappled with in writing this guide was "Who is it for?" If it is for program administrators, academics, funders, or policy makers, shouldn't it be written in a somewhat formal, academic style? If it's for teachers and practitioners, shouldn't it be written in a more popular style, with greater focus on method and practice?

We concluded that the book should be intentionally and explicitly for both. It's important for teachers to have an understanding of where their work fits in the bigger picture of educational policy and to have a conceptual framework to guide practice. It's also important for policy makers and program administrators to have a concrete sense of day-to-day classroom life. All too often, administrators, academics, and practitioners travel in separate circles, meeting only over proposals, budgets, and test scores. This book is intended to help bridge that gap by integrating research findings and accounts of teachers' experiences, theoretical developments and practical issues.

The Book's Structure

The structure of the book mirrors the curriculum development process. Chapter 1 starts by elaborating the *conceptual framework* for a participatory approach, with an explanation of the principles and rationale for participatory literacy education. Chapter 2 examines *structural issues* in setting up programs in terms of their implications for curriculum development and classroom dynamics. Moving into the classroom, Chapters 3 and 4 present an *overview* of the curriculum development process and ways of *finding student issues;* Chapter 5 discusses participatory tools for developing language, literacy, and critical thinking around themes, and Chapter 6 addresses *issues* that arise in putting the model into practice. Chapter 7 explores ways of using literacy to take *action for change* both inside and outside the classroom. An analysis of different perspectives on *evaluation* and options for alternative, participatory evaluation are presented in Chapter 8. The book concludes with implications for the field of adult ESL/ literacy as a whole based on our work. The list of Resources at the end includes books, curriculum guides, articles, and newsletters for teachers interested in pursuing a participatory approach to adult ESL/literacy and materials that can be used in the classroom (both traditional ESL texts and alternative resources).

How the Book Can Best Be Used

Whatever conclusions we came to in our own work were the result of a group process, and our sense is that *this book can best be utilized by a group of people reading and reacting to it together.* This means that teachers need time to meet together regularly; an essential component of any participatory adult literacy program is ongoing staff development. We hope that this guide will be used in that kind of a setting, as a catalyst for groups implementing their own programs. The group exercises included in it serve two functions: first, to facilitate the development of your own group process, examining your assumptions about literacy, sharing experience, and adapting the model to your own conditions; and second, to model the kind of exercises you might want to do with students.

We don't expect that anyone will read *Making Meaning, Making Change* linearly, from beginning to end, but rather that readers will use it as a resource, going back and forth between the ideas presented here and practice, selecting and experimenting with sections as they become relevant in particular contexts.

Our hope is that you will adapt *Making Meaning, Making Change* to your own realities by using it interactively, evaluating what we say in light of your experiences, settings, and values, and taking from it what is relevant to your context. The principles of participatory learning—sharing ideas and working out ways of putting them into practice collaboratively—apply as much to educators as to students. There are structured exercises throughout the guide to facilitate this kind of interaction, so that you can draw out your own experience and ideas as a reference point for what you read.

1 What Is a Participatory Approach to Curriculum Development?

In order to frame your thinking about approaches to curriculum before reading this chapter, take fifteen minutes to write about a positive memory you have of a school experience. Then do the same for a negative school experience. If you are working in a group, compare the experiences you wrote about:

♦ *What do the positive experiences have in common?*
♦ *What do the negative experiences have in common?*
♦ *What elements seem to characterize the positive/negative learning experiences?*
♦ *What generalizations can you make about positive and negative learning experiences, environments, and processes?*
♦ *What implications do these observations have for teaching?*

Now take some time to answer the questions about curriculum development below. The purpose here is to articulate your past or current practice in order to begin thinking and talking about the spectrum of approaches to developing curriculum that you are already familiar with. If you are working with a group, discuss your answers together: First describe what you do and then talk about how you feel about it (what you like or don't like about the process, advantages or disadvantages of doing things that way, and any concerns that have arisen out of this experience).

Your Practice...

1. What are the goals of the program?
♦ What would count as success?
♦ What are the funders' and administrators' hopes for the students?
♦ What are the teachers' hopes for the students?
♦ What are the students' hopes for themselves?

2. How is a needs assessment done?
♦ Who does it? When is it done?
♦ If teachers are not involved, what information do they get ?
♦ On what basis are students placed in classes?

3. How is the content of your curriculum determined?
♦ Who decides what is to be covered?
♦ What is the organizing principle of the curriculum (grammar? competencies? survival topics? situations?)
♦ On what basis are topics/grammar points/competencies chosen?
♦ When is curriculum content determined?
♦ What is the role of each of the following in deciding content and shaping the syllabus: funders, administrators, teachers, students?

4. How are classroom processes, activities, and materials determined?
♦ Who decides what students will do and how they will do it?
♦ What kinds of materials and activities are used?
♦ How are they selected or designed? When are they chosen?
♦ How are lessons planned?
♦ Is instruction mainly individual, small group, or whole group?
♦ What does the teacher do if the class gets side-tracked from the plan?

5. What is the teacher's role in the classroom?
♦ What does the teacher do before, during, and after class?
♦ How do the students view the teacher's role?
♦ What does the teacher do about problems in class?

6. What is the students' role in the classroom?
♦ To what extent do students decide how and what the class will study?
♦ To what extent do they select or create materials?
♦ What is their role in evaluation of their learning?

7. How are the outcomes determined?
♦ What kinds of outcomes are considered important?
♦ Who decides what possible/acceptable outcomes are?
♦ How is evaluation (individual, class, and program) done?

Our Practice...

As curriculum theorists point out, every approach to curriculum development reflects a certain view of learners and learning. Very often, these views are implicit in the way curriculum is developed and structured, in the choices about curriculum content and goals, and in the patterning of social relations in the classroom.

We started our own work in the Family Literacy Project by trying to get a sense of the range of approaches and models that others had developed for similar programs. While we brought a wealth of experience teaching adult ESL and literacy in a variety of contexts (from refugee camps to workplace and community-based programs), none of us had worked in a family literacy program before. Thus, we felt that it would be important to situate our work within the broader framework of existing research and conceptualizations of family literacy, to understand on the one hand what the research had to say about how families contribute to literacy development and, on the other, how programs were designed to promote this development. We wanted to examine the range of answers to questions like those posed above, looking not just at program designs but at the assumptions they were based on and the rationale that informed them. This led us to step back and ask a set of questions about the social context of family literacy programming itself:

♦ Why is family literacy becoming such a popular trend now?
♦ What models are now being used to involve English and language minority families in children's literacy development?
♦ What assumptions are these models based on?
♦ What does the research say about how families contribute to the literacy development of children?
♦ How do the families' contributions vary according to class and culture?
♦ What alternatives are there to the predominant models?

We embarked on this investigation process by doing three things:

1. reviewing studies of home literacy contexts and family contributions to literacy development of children from different classes and cultures (ethnographic research);
2. looking at existing family literacy program models; and, perhaps most importantly,
3. learning from our students, investigating with them their own family literacycontexts.

While this is not the place to present an in-depth analysis of our findings, there are several points that are critical for understanding our rationale in pursuing a participatory approach to curriculum development. (See Auerbach, 1989b, for a fuller analysis of these questions).

Most importantly, what we found was that existing programs were often not informed by research findings. The evidence about family contributions to literacy acquisition and implications for practice pointed in one direction while the predominant approach to program design pointed in another.

On the one hand, programs are often based on the assumption that the homes of low-income, minority, and ESL students are "literacy impoverished," with limited reading material, parents who don't read, don't value literacy, and don't provide support for their children's literacy development. Based on this notion of family deficit, program goals are often framed in terms of transforming home contexts into sites for mainstream literacy interactions; parents are taught to do specific school-like literacy tasks with their children and to interact with the schools on the schools' terms. Curricula focus on giving parents instruction in becoming home tutors, training in "effective parenting," and information on the culture of American schooling. In this "transmission of school practices" model, the direction is from the schools to the families.

On the other hand, studies of low-income, minority, and immigrant families show that they often use literacy for a wide variety of purposes, have homes filled with print, and not only value literacy, but see it as the key to mobility. Even parents with little education and limited literacy support their children's literacy development in a variety of ways (Chall & Snow, 1982; Delgado-Gaitan, 1987; Taylor & Dorsey-Gaines, 1988). When we investigated family interactions around literacy with our students, we found a picture of mutual support and sharing of strengths as the following examples show.

> I help my kids.
> I teach them good things.
> I play with them. I protect
> them. I correct them.
> My kids bring me things.
> My kids will teach me English.
> My kids make me happy.
> Maybe they will take care of me.
>
> Gebre Goso

> I help my kids by staying
> together with them. By talking to
> them. I help them by confronting
> them and telling them whats wrong
> or right. Just as they do me.
> I help them when they need a
> favor or money just as they do me.
> It's just like you scratch my
> back I scratch your back with
> my family.
>
> Maria Bento

Interestingly, the way the second piece was written itself exemplifies the "you scratch my back, I'll scratch yours" dynamic in this family: The mother is herself a beginning ESL student with minimal first language literacy skills. She collaborated with her daughter in a language experience process to produce this piece. The mother told the daughter what she wanted to say and the daughter helped the mother to write it.

Further, studies of the homes of successful readers found that interactions around print varied greatly. No specific school-like instructional practices accounted for literacy acquisition; rather, literacy was integrated in a socially significant way into many aspects of family life and developed to the extent that it was a tool for addressing needs and issues of importance for the family. Thus, Taylor (1983) concludes:

> The approach that has been taken in recent years has been to develop parent education programmes which very often provide parents with a battery of specific activities which are designed to teach reading, and yet very little available evidence suggests that parents with children who read without difficulty actually undertake such 'teaching' on a regular basis. The present study suggests that there

are great variations in approaches the parents have evolved in working with their children and that the thread that unites the families is the recognition that learning to read takes place on a daily basis as part of everyday life. (p. 101)

The following piece, written by a student, Rosa, while she was in a primarily grammar-based classroom, is a response to the teacher's exasperated query about why no one had done their homework exercises:

Why I Didn't Do the Homework

Because the phone is ringing
    the door is noking
    the kid is yumping
    the food is burning
    time runs fast.

Implicit in this response is a plea for the teacher to understand the complex context of the student's life: She is more than a student—she is a parent, wife, cook, neighbor, and community member, trying to balance the demands of these many roles. Formal decontextualized homework becomes one more burden that seems in conflict with the demands of daily living. It doesn't always fit in or make sense. The following piece, written by the same student when she was in a family literacy class where the teacher invited students to explore and write about the dynamics of language choice in their families, uses the home context as content for writing, focusing on the issues that the student is involved with in her daily life.

At Home

I talk to my kids about school
I ask...¿Como se portaron?
They say very good.
I continue in ask
about the food...and the homework.
they speak to me in english....
I say I am sorry....
Yo no entendí nada; por favor háblame
en español... The older boy says OK..OK.
You study english you are supposed to
understand. They repeat again to me
slowly and more *clearly*. Yo les digo...
Muchas gracias.... I love you.
They are 4, 6 and 10 years old.

Here literacy no longer seems in opposition to the student's concerns but is a tool for reflecting and acting on them. With these two pieces, Rosa's message here is clear: It is important to connect what happens inside the classroom with what happens outside the classroom so that literacy can become a tool for making changes in students' lives.

Taken together, this evidence suggested to us a very different model from the predominant transmission of school practices model: a model that acknowledges family strengths; investigates with students family contexts for literacy usage, attitudes and practices; and explores with students possibilities for change. Rather than proceeding from the schools to the families, the direction of this model is from the families and communities to the schools. Parents' roles, thus, are no longer defined in terms of implementing school goals or practices, but rather in terms of using literacy as a tool to deal with issues in their own daily reality. The premise here is that literacy will become socially significant in family life (and thus provide a context conducive to children's literacy acquisition) when participants in family literacy programs become critical readers of their own social contexts and authors of the changes they hope to make. The approach to curriculum development, thus, must be context-specific, grounded in the particular realities of each group of participants, and based on a collaborative investigation of critical issues in family and community life. As these issues emerge, they are explored and transformed into content-based literacy work so that literacy can, in turn, become a tool for making change in the conditions of students' lives. The two pieces on the previous page by Rosa illustrate the impact on student literacy development of these two differing approaches to literacy curriculum development.

While we arrived at our analysis within the context of a family literacy project, there are two lessons that are generalizable to other adult literacy contexts:

1. In order to develop a conceptual basis for any project, *it is important to understand the social context in which the project itself takes place*: why the project is being funded, what assumptions it rests on, whose interests it serves, whose agenda is driving it, how it views learners, etc.

2. The key to successful literacy acquisition is the extent to which literacy is rooted in and integrally related to issues of importance in learners' lives. It is this second claim that we will explore further in the rest of this chapter. We will start by stepping back to get a broad picture of traditional and participatory approaches to curriculum development, going on to examine in more detail some of the characteristics of a traditional approach and the rationale for and characteristics of a participatory approach, and concluding with general principles of participatory curriculum development.

Two Approaches to Curriculum Development: The Big Picture

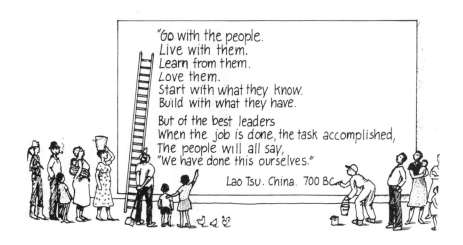

"Go with the people.
Live with them.
Learn from them.
Love them.
Start with what they know.
Build with what they have.

But of the best leaders
When the job is done, the task accomplished,
The people will all say,
"We have done this ourselves."

Lao Tsu. China. 700 BC

Reprinted by permission of SWAPO Literacy Campaign.

This graphic comes from the *Literacy Promoter's Handbook* (SWAPO Literacy Campaign, 1986, p. 6), a guide for Namibian literacy workers. Although the quote was originally written almost three thousand years ago, and is taken here from materials being used in a third world setting, the message is a universal one, fully relevant to our work with immigrants and refugees in a North American context. The message is a simple one: that people learn best when learning starts with what they already know, builds on their strengths, engages them in the learning process, and enables them to accomplish something they want to accomplish. This is the essence of a participatory approach. The only thing astounding about this approach is that it is not the norm; in fact, it is diametrically opposed to the way that many of us have been taught, and, as the following pages (excerpted from the same manual, pp. 3-4) indicate, differs from the "old" methods used in many adult literacy settings.

As you read the next few pages, think about how each of the methods presented relates to your own learning and teaching experiences. Which method is closest to the way you learned (what you wrote about at the beginning of this chapter)? Which is closest to teaching approaches you're familiar with?

Reprinted by permission of SWAPO Literacy Campaign.

Reprinted by permission of SWAPO Literacy Campaign.

What Characterizes a More Traditional, Ends-Means Approach?

One way to explain a participatory approach to ESL literacy is to contrast it with the more familiar ends-means approach in which experts identify a body of knowledge to be covered during a specified time period (ends) and provide a plan (means) for meeting predetermined objectives before instruction begins. Of course, the danger of setting up such a contrast is that it creates a kind of polarization that may not correspond to the lived experience of practitioners. Most programs are neither purely traditional nor purely participatory, but draw on elements of each and lie somewhere on a continuum between the two extremes. As such, the contrast oversimplifies reality. Nevertheless, it serves a function: It should be seen not so much as a system for categorizing or labeling programs, but rather as a tool for framing thinking about possibilities and situating programs along a continuum. Having said this, I now proceed with the oversimplified description of an ends-means approach!

The curriculum development process starts with experts identifying and describing a body of knowledge to be covered (as in the case of the Texas Adult Performance Level Study [APL] in which university-based researchers surveyed literacy usage in a wide variety of contexts, identifying 65 competencies that they claimed were necessary for "successful functioning in society"). Often this is done by consulting those in the mainstream society who will be interacting with the learner (e.g., employers or school personnel) in order to determine their expectations: what they need, hope, or expect the learner to be able to do as a result of instruction. The results of the investigation process then determine what gets taught (thus, the APL Study became the basis for competency-based ESL texts and curricula).

Content, in this view, derives from this externally defined body of knowledge (whether it be in the form of grammar, language use, cultural information, life skills, or competencies). This received content is broken down into parts according to topic, function, or form, with the resulting syllabus becoming a kind of blueprint or roadmap for instruction. The recent concern with accountability has led to very detailed specification of content, linguistic/behavioral tasks, outcomes, and performance standards.

Needs assessment very often follows the formulation of the syllabus. Thus, it is done a priori, as a *precondition* to instruction, to determine for the purposes of placement which skills students lack. In many cases, assessment is done by someone other than the teacher and results are presented to the teacher in quantified form, with no account of the assessment interaction itself. Often, assessment data inform instruction only to the extent that they serve as a baseline against which progress is measured. Sometimes (e.g., in competency-based ESL), teaching specifically targets weaknesses identified in pretesting and considers any teaching not related to these points to be deviations that don't count.

The teachers' role in this process is to transmit skills and knowledge; the *students' role* is to receive knowledge. Thus, the teacher is the knower and the student is the knowee. Because learning is defined as the acquisition of skills or knowledge, it is seen to be primarily an individual process, with each learner proceeding at his/her own pace, accumulating skills/knowledge with assistance from the teacher. Although there may be flexibility in terms of materials or methods for attaining the prespecified objectives, any classroom activity not directed at meeting these objectives is considered a deviation.

Outcomes are also measured against these predetermined objectives. Teachers are evaluated in terms of how well they cover the syllabus. Students are evaluated in terms of gains between pretesting and posttesting. Great stress is placed on quantification of progress and objectivity of assessment. Further, outcomes must be correlated with objectives; this means that predictability is valued. Funding is often contingent on meeting goals that have been specified before students have been admitted. Thus, to the program, projected *results* shape recruitment: Only those students who are likely to meet predetermined outcomes are accepted.

Thus, in this approach, the educator/expert does most of the work of naming the reality, determining the needs and objectives, developing the educational plan, providing the materials, and evaluating the outcomes. As a result, according to Freire (1981), the educator acts as a *problem-solver* for the student, "curing" the student by prescribing or transmitting educational medicine (in the form of skills, behaviors, or competencies), with the result that the student's voice is silenced.

Quite a literal example of this silencing took place in a factory-based ESL class that I observed several years ago. I arrived early and found the students, Portuguese women who had been in this country for many years, engaged in an animated and angry discussion of something that had happened to one of them that day: After eight years on the job, she had suddenly been shifted from an hourly rate job to a piece-rate job in violation of the union contract. The teacher, who herself was Portuguese, joined the discussion. Passionate debate ranged from why the boss had done this, to what the woman could do and how the others might help. Suddenly the teacher looked at her watch and said it was time to start class. She had prepared a lesson on calling in sick, after a careful needs assessment of the kinds of language the women needed for the workplace. What followed was a solid hour of silence, with the women alternately looking out the window, at their shoes, and at the clock.

This episode represents more than just missing a teachable moment; it represents a stance toward education. The teacher felt she had to stick to her lesson; it was what she was "supposed to do" and if she had allowed the students to keep talking about what had happened at work, she said she would have felt guilty. She was a committed person who had spent long hours doing a needs assessment and preparing detailed lesson plans on the skills her students needed to fit into the workplace. But by making the decision for her students, she assumed control of the situation, robbing them of the chance to participate in directing their own learning.

A Participatory Approach: the Emergent Curriculum

In contrast to the ends-means approach, a curriculum that aims to be centered on issues of importance to participants must be tailored to each group of students. It can't be developed before the educator ever comes in contact with the class, but rather has to be built on the particular conditions, concerns, and contributions of specific groups of participants at a particular point in time.

A host of factors must be taken into account: Are participants from the same language group or different ones? Are they working or on welfare? What are the ages of their children? Do they live in public housing? The list goes on, but the point is that educators can't know the specific concerns of any group until they come in contact with them. There may be a set of generic issues—issues that are common and predictable for most immigrants and refugees in this country—but it isn't possible to know which of these will be resonant issues for any given group at a given point in time. The only way to find out what a particular group is concerned about, how they already use literacy, and how they might use it to address these concerns, is to investigate the social context of their lives with them.

Clearly, this approach demands a fundamental reconceptualization of curriculum development. Whereas, in the traditional approach, the teacher walks into the classroom armed with a predetermined set of objectives or outcomes, syllabus, lesson plans, and texts, in a participatory approach the curriculum *emerges* as a result of an ongoing, collaborative investigation of critical themes in students' lives. But where does this leave the teacher? Contrary to some misconceptions, it doesn't mean that the teacher goes into the classroom empty-handed, waiting for issues to fall from the sky. *A participatory approach provides the teacher with a structured process for developing context-specific curricula, involving students at every step of the way*. To implement this process, the educator needs four things:

1. a clear *conceptualization* of the rationale for the approach (what this chapter hopes to provide);
2. an *overview of the process* (elaborated in Chapter 3);
3. a set of *tools and procedures* for finding and developing student themes into literacy work (Chapters 4 and 5); and
4. a set of *resources* to draw on in implementing the approach, including materials and coworkers to talk to about the process as it develops (a list of resources is included at the end of the book).

Rationale for a Participatory Approach

The "why" for participatory literacy comes from adult learning theory, second language acquisition theory, and literacy theory, each of which is touched on only briefly here.

Adult Learning Theory. A central concept in adult learning theory is *self-directed learning*. As Knowles (1984) and others have pointed out, adult education is most effective when it is experience-centered, related to learners' real needs, and directed by learners themselves. Rather than abstract, decontextualized instruction focusing on isolated skills or generic topics, content must be contextualized in terms of student-determined interests and goals. It must be related in a meaningful way to the students' everyday reality and useful in enabling students to achieve their own purposes. Thus, adult learning theory supports the view that learners must be involved in determining both the content and direction of their education.

Second Language Acquisition (SLA) Theory. This concern with context and meaning are reflected in SLA theory. In the past twenty years, there has been a paradigm shift away from grammar-based and behavioral approaches (both of which are form-centered in orientation) toward *meaning-centered* approaches to English as a Second Language (ESL). Language is no longer seen only as a system of rules or behaviors that have an autonomous existence independent of their usage. The notion of *communicative competence* implies that it is not enough to know the grammar of a language; it is necessary also to know appropriate forms to use as the context changes. According to this view, both grammatical and sociolinguistic knowledge are acquired in the process of meaningful interaction in a range of settings, with a range of purposes, and participants. Real communication, accompanied by appropriate feedback that subordinates form to the elaboration of meaning, is key for language learning.

It is the teachers' task to create contexts for this type of communicative activity to take place. One of the means for creating such contexts is through *content-based* instruction: Contexts that focus on the exchange and creation of substantive information provide opportunities to link language acquisition with cognitive development. Further, *cooperative learning through peer interaction* provides students with greater opportunity to use language than teacher-centered participant structures; in addition, task- or problem-oriented activities provide a context for authentic dialogue and purposeful language use.

Literacy Theory. Central to recent developments in literacy theory is the notion that literacy practices, like language, are variable, context-dependent, and culture-specific. Until recently, literacy was seen as a monolithic set of neutral skills existing independently of how or where they're used. Literacy was seen to have certain inherent qualities that inevitably led to higher order cognitive processing (e.g., logical thinking) and economic advancement (see Gee, 1986, for a review of these perspectives).

However, studies of the real-world uses of literacy and literacy acquisition in different settings have revealed that the ways people read and write vary according to the task, the situation, the purpose, and the relationship between reader, writer, and setting. Further, the particular practices and beliefs about literacy for a given society depend on a range of cultural, social, and political factors. This research refutes claims made for literacy, showing that logical thinking is a consequence not of literacy per se but of how it is taught; economic advancement is determined more by race, ethnicity, and class than by literacy level (see Gee, 1986, for a comprehensive review of recent research supporting this analysis). Heath's (1983) work showed that although different communities use different literacy practices, those of middle-class communities are most like those of schools; and because authority is vested in those with mainstream ways (i.e., the ways of the school), children from middle-class communities had an advantage. This advantage has more to do with power relationships than with any inherent qualities of their particular literacy practices.

Street (1984) argues that it is no accident that literacy has traditionally been viewed as a unitary phenomenon, with inherent qualities and consequences. He argues that this view of literacy is a way of privileging one group's "ways with words" over others'. Recognizing only one culture-specific set of literacy practices, namely those taught and used in school (what Street calls "western essay-text literacy"), and elevating it to universal status, serves to maintain the dominance of those who use it. Its status comes not from its inherent features, but from its relation to the social order, because of who owns and has access to it. Street, Heath, and others argue that it must be explicitly acknowledged that each view of literacy reflects a particular ideological perspective. The traditional view justifies the status quo by valuing certain literacy practices over others; the sociocontextual view opens the door to changes in power relations by recognizing the legitimacy of diverse literacy practices.

A number of studies exploring the implications of this perspective for literacy instruction have appeared recently (again, see Gee, 1986 and Heath, 1983). Heath and Branscombe (1985), for example, suggest teaching students to become ethnographers of their own literacy communities, involving them in the process of investigating language and literacy usage. Their work with middle school students showed that when students become literacy researchers, exploring literacy beliefs and practices in their own families and communities, they make tremendous literacy gains. This study suggests that the process of observing, collecting, recording, and analyzing data about language and literacy use in itself facilitates literacy acquisition because *literacy is both the instrument and the object of study*. As we embarked on our project, we tried to identify features that characterized Heath and Branscombe's approach to literacy instruction, and came up with the following guidelines (implementation of these guidelines is discussed in Chapter 3):

Guidelines for Literacy Instruction

1. Create a literate classroom environment.
♦ Permeate the atmosphere with talk about language and literacy use.
♦ Constantly link reading and writing to students' daily lives.
♦ Treat students as though they are avid readers and writers.

2. Make literacy classroom activities real, student-centered, and communicative.
♦ Start with personal writing: autobiographical, student-initiated topics.
♦ Use literacy for real purposes and audiences (e.g., set up letter-writing teams).

3. Connect content inside the the class to the community outside.
♦ Have students investigate language, literacy, and variability of usage.
♦ Identify contexts and purposes for literacy practices.

4. Develop literate practices through research in which students:
♦ collect data (participant observation, interviews, reading inventories);
♦ record data (field notes, taping, transcribing);
♦ analyze data (finding patterns, comparing);
♦ report on the analysis and present findings; and
♦ establish a community of researchers for responding, criticizing, refining, and producing a revised analysis.

The recent theoretical developments discussed above suggest that instruction must include explicit discussion of literacy learning itself. This means (a) involving learners in the investigation of their own literacy practices; (b) critically analyzing with learners how the educational system has shaped their development, self-image, and possibilities by devaluing their knowledge and promoting one culture-specific norm at the expense of others; and (c) involving students in determining their own purposes, rather than prescribing practices for them.

The work of Brazilian educator Paulo Freire is perhaps the most important inspiration for a participatory approach to ESL. His approach, developed in the

1950s during a literacy campaign among peasants and slum-dwellers in Brazil, involved engaging learners in dialogue about key words representing problematic issues in their lives in order to foster critical analysis of the issues. These dialogues became the basis for literacy development and action for change. What was significant about Freire's work was his insistence on linking literacy to social change. As he says, "reading the word" and "reading the world" go hand in hand: Literacy education is meaningful to the extent that it engages learners in reflecting on their relationship to the world they live in and provides them a means to shape that world (Freire & Macedo, 1987). Freire claims that every curriculum reflects a particular view of the world, whether or not it is explicitly acknowledged. Thus, education is never neutral. It can either serve to perpetuate existing social relations or to challenge them.

> Education either functions as an instrument which is used to facilitate the integration...into the logic of the present system and bring about conformity to it, or it becomes the "practice of freedom," the means by which men and women deal critically and creatively with reality and discover how to participate in the transformation of their world. (Freire, 1970, p. 15)

Freire argues that both the content and the processes of traditional adult literacy perpetuate the marginalization of learners. When literacy is taught as a collection of decontextualized, meaningless skills, starting with letters and sounds divorced from any significance in learners' lives, they cannot use their minds or bring anything to the learning process, and therefore become objects of instruction. Students are seen as lacking the skills and behaviors needed to function in the society as it exists; the curriculum focuses on transferring knowledge that will help students fit in. Freire calls this the "banking model" of education: Learners are seen as empty vessels, devoid of any knowledge, and the educators' job is to fill the empty accounts by making deposits of knowledge. The learners thus become passive recipients of prepackaged and predetermined curriculum content. The classroom processes themselves are disempowering because they rehearse students for submissive roles in the social order outside the classroom. As Freire (1970) says, this kind of curriculum is domesticating in that it tames people into uncritical acceptance of things as they are, discouraging them from actively challenging the forces that keep them marginalized.

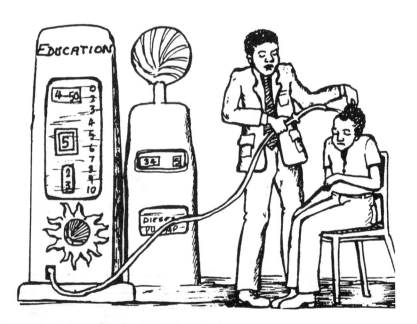

From *Training for Transformation, Book 1* (p. 103) by A. Hope and S. Timmel, 1984, Giveru, Zimbabwe: Mambo Press. Reprinted by permission.

In contrast to this domesticating education, Freire proposes a model whose goal is to enable learners to become active participants in shaping their own realities. Both the content and processes of this model invite learners to become the subjects of their own education. Content centers on problematic issues from their lives, so literacy is immediately relevant and engaging. Because this reality is problematized (presented in all its complexity, without predetermined solutions), participants become the creators rather than the recipients of knowledge. They engage in a process of reflection and dialogue, developing both an understanding of the root causes of the problem and generating their own alternatives for addressing it. Literacy learning becomes a context for thinking critically about social issues in a process that Freire calls "conscientization." "Learners enter into the process of learning not by acquiring facts [skills, competencies] but by constructing their reality in social exchange with others" (Auerbach & Wallerstein, 1987, p.1). This radically transforms their relation to education, making them subjects of their own learning; at the same time, because literacy becomes a tool for addressing problems, it transforms their relation to the world, making them subjects of their own history. Education thus is part of a liberating process rather than a domesticating one. Freire's four-part process for putting this theory into practice can be characterized as follows:

Overview of Freire's Curriculum Development Process

1. The listening phase. During this time, the educator immerses him or herself in the community of the students, becoming intimately familiar with their daily reality. Through this investigation process, the educator identifies critical social issues from students' lives and selects a core group of shared issues that become the backbone of the literacy curriculum. Issues are selected on the basis of their evocative power—the extent to which they trigger strong emotional responses. The educator then distills these themes into codes or codifications—abstracted representations in graphic form of the issues, depicted so that they are depersonalized and objective but immediately recognizable. Problems are presented in a two-sided way so that no solution or predetermined interpretation is implied. For each theme, a generative (key) word is selected that both reflects the loaded issue and has a regular syllable structure.

2. The dialogue phase. Learners work together in dialogue circles, reflecting on the codes; the facilitator/teacher guides their dialogue through steps moving from literal interpretation of the code, to linking it to personal conditions and situations, to reflecting on its root causes and considering alternative ways of addressing the problem. Through this conscientization process, participants deepen their understanding of the conditions shaping their lives. The group nature of this process is critical: Participants each contribute their interpretations and collectively arrive at an analysis of the situation; they share experiences and ideas in order to generate their own alternatives for action.

3. The decoding and recoding phase. Once students have "read the world" of a generative word, they move on to "reading the word" itself, grappling with syllable structure. The process moves from analyzing the word in terms of its meaning in participants' lives, to analyzing it linguistically, breaking it into syllables that are then recombined to make new words, and new meanings.

4. The action phase. The final phase entails doing something in the real world as a result of the reflection and dialogue. In Freire's case, the literacy campaign led peasants and slum-dwellers to become active participants in the political process. On a more limited scale, the point of the action phase is to return to the problem that inspired the literacy work and work to change the conditions that gave rise to it.

Beyond Freire

For the past three decades, educators around the world have been working to put Freire's vision of "education for transformation" into practice. Early attempts often focused on struggling to transpose Freire's pedagogy into different contexts in a literal way; however, because his work grew out of specific conditions, took place in a third world country, was developed for a syllabically regular language, and was part of a movement for social change, this kind of literal translation was often not possible, causing some practitioners to become discouraged or to question its applicability to their situation. However, over time, it became clear that this kind of transposition of methodology was neither the intention nor the spirit of Freire's approach. Rather, practitioners realized that they had to constantly reinvent Freire for their own contexts, taking from his work the underlying outlook but developing tools to implement it according to their own situations. Thus, over the past twenty years, Freire's vision has been adapted for second language, workplace, health, and peace education internationally. The popular education and participatory research movements have both been influenced by Freire. His ideas have been widely adapted for ESL with the development of Wallerstein's (1983) problem-posing approach and the participatory ESL movement in Canada.

The challenge for anyone trying to apply a Freirean perspective is to figure out what is and what isn't relevant to a given context. The brief summary outlined here is by no means a prescription for practice. As the body of Freire-inspired practice grows, there have been inevitable refinements, reformulations, and challenges to both the form and content of Freire's ideas. Key among these is expansion of the learners' role in the curriculum development process; specifically, where Freire suggested that the educator undertake a period of investigation and identification of themes before instruction begins, others have moved toward a process of identifying themes through dialogue with participants, as part of the instructional process. In addition, rather than focusing on a single method (moving from code to dialogue to generative word to syllabification to creating new words and moving toward action), others have expanded the range of tools and processes for exploring issues, with student involvement in the production of material. Further, many have questioned the notion that the teacher's role is to facilitate conscientization and analytical thinking because it implies that the teacher has a more developed understanding than the students. The process of trying to redefine roles in the classroom has been as much a learning process for teacher-learners as for student-learners. The following passage is an adult basic education (ABE) teacher's explanation of how her thinking developed on this issue.

> Up to a year and a half ago, I was a teacher because I thought people needed to think more critically about the social conditioning of their personal experience, to look underneath the myths that obscure our vision of what's going on in our lives and the world...
>
> But the problem this notion began to raise for me is that the women where I worked often did view reality with a critical consciousness; they quite often did see the social conditioning of their own lives. John Gwaltney, in *Drylongso: A Self Portrait of Black America*, said that "principled survival is a preeminently analytical process." A woman in one class once talked about how you have to lie to your caseworker to squeeze what you need out of welfare, but that having to lie in front of your children "takes away your freedom." Deciding which to trade off—your right to demonstrate your real integrity to your child, or getting her a decent looking coat so she doesn't feel humiliated at school—knowing that freedom is what hangs in the balance, is a "preeminently analytical process..."
>
> When I first wrote the paragraph above, I wondered if I should take it out. I shouldn't *have* to remind myself that the women I work with think analytically. But I have to painfully admit that sometimes my eyes aren't open to it....

I also began to realize that within the framework I'd used, there wasn't a place for me, as a teacher, with which I was comfortable. The role it left me was that of a facilitator whose consciousness was already raised, helping other people to raise theirs. I was beginning to see that I couldn't reconcile that role with the reality of who the women in my classes really were. I also started to see how that premise didn't fit with the fact that my own awareness of many things still needed raising, or that even when my awareness of an issue is high, my actions don't always match it. In sum, I couldn't reconcile this role with the view I wanted to have of myself as a co-learner..." (Martin, 1989, pp. 5-6.)

Reprinted by permission of the author.

It is the accumulated body of practice based on Freire's work that is the real inspiration for a participatory approach. While Freire's work is a starting point, the broadened perspective that has emerged through teachers sharing experiences in conferences, in written accounts of their practice, and in informal networks is the essence of participatory education.

What Characterizes a Participatory Approach?

Going back to our comparison (polarization!) between an ends-means approach and a participatory approach, we can see how they differ in terms of essential features. Most importantly, in a participatory approach, teachers and students work together to decide what to focus on in class and how to proceed, rather than having educators/experts deciding for them.

The curriculum development process involves students at every step of the way, from needs assessment through evaluation. Students are assumed to be the experts on their own reality and very much involved in researching that reality with teachers. This collaborative investigation of what is important to students is at the heart of the instructional process, the direction of which is *from the students to the curriculum* rather than *from the curriculum to the students*. In place of a static body of knowledge defined by outside experts, students and teachers have a set of principles and processes to guide their own selection of content and production of knowledge. Not only are students involved in deciding *what* is to be done, they are involved in deciding *how* to do it; as they participate increasingly in creating and producing their own forms and materials (drawings, photos, drama, stories, music), they take more control of the learning process.

Learning is seen to be a collective process, where participants share and analyze experiences together in order to address concerns, relying on each others' strengths and resources rather than addressing problems individually or relying on outside experts to solve them.

Needs assessment is an ongoing process, integrated into classroom interaction rather than preceding instruction. Of course, students are grouped according to certain criteria (which may include literacy level, interests, native language, age of children, etc.). However, rather than serving as a baseline against which to assess progress in posttesting, ongoing needs analysis is used as the basis for curriculum development; analyzing needs, interests, strengths, and concerns is very much part of the process of acquiring control over one's own learning and is therefore an important part of the students' work. If, as we said earlier, family literacy is seen as a social process shaped by a host of factors inside and outside the family (family roles, housing conditions, work, childcare, etc.), one of the important functions of the needs analysis is to engage students in examining their own contexts, identifying factors and dynamics that shape their environment so they can begin to change it.

Content in this approach emerges through the ongoing classroom interaction. With no received body of knowledge to be covered or transmitted, an important part of participatory curriculum development is transferring the tools for the production of knowledge to the students. This means they have to be involved not only in determining content but in explicitly reflecting on what counts as knowledge, on how learning takes place, and on their own roles in the process. As Barndt (1986) says, students discover their own knowledge, create new knowledge and act on this knowledge. The bank from which content is drawn is the social reality of students' lives: It may range from the immediate context of the classroom itself to family or community contexts to broader political issues; it may include explicit discussion about literacy practices and literacy acquisition. This doesn't mean, however, that nothing can be prepared in advance. As Chapters 3, 4, 5, and 6 will show, teachers can draw on prior experience in terms of familiarity with potential issues, catalysts to trigger exploration of issues with each group of students, tools to develop literacy around these themes, and resources to deepen the analysis of issues as they arise. Many centers, for example, compile files, with copies of all class materials around particular themes that teachers can draw from if and when those themes arise in class.

Choices about content are made collaboratively through "negotiated selection from these open-ended banks, guided by the curriculum principles" (Candlin, 1984). The syllabus, in this view, is more of a *retroactive account* than a blueprint or roadmap; it is a syllabus of *how* rather than a syllabus of *what* (Candlin, 1984). Again, this doesn't mean that the teacher walks into the class with no plan; rather, it means that the actual syllabus is an account of the interaction between the plan and the reality (what happened when the teacher tried to implement it). As Candlin (1984) says, "It is only from the tension between classroom action and curriculum guidelines...that we can expect innovation. It is this tension which can drive curricula forward, maintaining their relevance to the society of the classroom and that of the world outside."

The teacher's role is to act as a *problem-poser*, facilitating the process of uncovering important issues and reflecting on them. Because students are experts on their own reality, the teacher is a co-learner. The teacher's stance is one of asking questions rather than providing answers or transmitting knowledge or skills; when the teacher does answer questions it is in the spirit of sharing information as one member of a group, rather than as the expert. Because the learning process is seen to be a collective, group process, the teacher's job is to draw out the experience and perspective of participants so that they can use their collective knowledge to address issues. The teacher does this by creating a context where students feel comfortable in sharing what's important to them, by providing structures for getting at their concerns, by re-presenting issues in a form that will facilitate dialogue, by helping to structure exploration of the issues, by modeling and presenting choices for learning activities, and by sharing his or her own experiences, knowledge, ideas, and opinions.

Outcomes cannot be predicted if content and processes are genuinely student-centered. The *unpredictability* of outcomes is valued in that it indicates participants have genuinely been involved in determining their objectives for themselves. As L. Stenhouse (in Candlin, 1984) says, "Education as induction into knowledge is successful to the extent that it makes the behavioral outcomes of the students *unpredictable*." Thus, rather than feeling guilty about deviating from the plan when unexpected issues surface, the teacher welcomes precisely this kind of occurrence as the meat of a participatory process and is able to respond to it.

Further, in a participatory approach, *qualitative* change is given as much or more weight as *quantitative* change because the primary goal is that students move toward being able to address real life concerns and take action; this means that being able to describe and analyze changes is more important than being able to count them. Whereas measurable changes in skill or grade levels are valued in an ends-means approach, the diversification of uses of literacy and the ability to make literacy meaningful in everday life are valued in a participatory approach. These changes are not easily measurable and may have no clearly observable behavioral manifestations.

This means that *subjective* as well as *objective* evidence of progress is valued in a participatory approach. Since many of the changes are internal and affective, students' own assessment of accomplishment is important. As a result, the notion of external objective evaluation is no longer sufficient; it is critical that students themselves be involved in the evaluation process both because of the valuable evidence they can provide and because their participation is part of the process of gaining control of their learning and their lives.

Finally, progress is seen to be *cumulative* and *cyclical* rather than occurring in discrete, linear steps. Evidence of learning may not show up within a pre-specified time frame or at the moment it is being evaluated. It may take months after a class ends for its impact to manifest itself. Thus, in a participatory approach, there is no expectation that students will attain predetermined objectives within mandated time periods. Rather, both language and literacy acquisition are allowed to develop at their own pace, without the attempt to collapse into a short time frame a process that takes first language/literacy learners years to accomplish.

As in the ends-means approach, both the content and processes of a participatory classroom rehearse people for life roles; however, in this case, classroom relations prepare people for changing social relations outside the classroom, rather than for fitting into someone else's agenda. The transformation of student-teacher roles serves as a model for changes in roles outside the classroom. As participants become involved in directing their own education, they explore and rehearse active participation in other areas of their lives.

What Do These Approaches Look Like in Practice?

In the context of family literacy work, these two approaches to curriculum development take very different forms. An assimilative, ends-means approach would instruct parents to conform to school expectations by extending school practices into the home, teaching about American school culture and modeling "appropriate" parental behavior. A critical, participatory approach, on the other hand, would explore existing parental concerns, expectations, and practices, evaluate and challenge school practices if necessary, and use literacy to influence these realities.

An example from one of Loren's classes illustrates the difference between how assimilative literacy and critical literacy model and prepare students for life roles. One day, a student brought to class a flyer from her daughter's school with a list of ways parents can help their children with homework. In an assimilative approach, the teacher might have gone over the flyer point by point, talking about what parents can do to help their kids. Instead, the teacher did something quite different. The class still read the flyer, but the reading was followed by questions like this: *Which of these things do you already do? Which would you like to do? Which do you think are ridiculous, impossible, or not useful?* and *What do you already do that's not listed in the flyer?* This way of framing the reading led to a discussion of cultural differences in perceptions of teachers' vs. parents' roles (some critical cultural analysis). In addition, the parents identified both their own strengths (what they already do to help their children) and new things that they would like to try. By relating the flyer to their own reality, looking at it in a broader social context, and exploring possibilities, they maintained a stance of independence and choice in the learning process. This simple prescriptive flyer became the basis for shaping some of their own alternatives.

Summing Up: Principles for Participatory Curriculum Development

1. *Students are engaged in curriculum development at every stage of the process.* Ideally, this means that students participate in identifying issues, generating content, producing materials, determining outcomes, and evaluating learning. Realizing this ideal is a slow, gradual process that involves moving back and forth between old and new ways of doing things and making the approach to curriculum itself explicit. Students' increasing participation fosters motivation and self-confidence.

2. *The classroom is a model; what happens inside the classroom shapes the possibilities outside the classroom.* Both *what* is learned (content) and *how* it is learned (processes) shape students' perceptions of their own possibilities and prepare them for particular ways of acting in the outside world. Classroom social relations are a microcosm of social relations beyond the classroom.

Making changes inside the classroom itself models a way of addressing issues and redefining roles outside the classroom.

3. The focus is on strengths, not inadequacies. Students are seen as experts on their own reality and, as such, are invited to believe in themselves. The content stresses their capacity to create new knowledge rather than reproduce or duplicate someone else's knowledge. This means investigating, validating and extending what participants can (and want to) do rather than stressing what they can't do or imposing what educators/experts think they should be doing.

4. The teacher's role is one of problem-poser rather than problem-solver. The teacher is not the one with answers, but the one who facilitates students' discovery of their own answers. The teacher catalyzes reflection on students' everyday reality. As concerns are identified, the teacher re-presents them to the class and guides students through an exploration process, contributing linguistic expertise while learning from the students' about their reality. "Everyone teaches, everyone learns." (Arnold, Barndt, & Burke, 1985, p.16). The group generates its own ways of addressing concerns through collective dialogue.

5. The content comes from the social context. For literacy to be relevant, what goes on inside the classroom must relate to students' lives outside the classroom; thus, the starting point is the concrete experience of the learner. Students develop literacy by reading, writing, and talking about social factors (like housing, work, or neighborhood safety) in their family and community contexts and, most importantly, about ways that they can shape these conditions.

6. Language, literacy and culture are explored as part of the content because they are important aspects of the context. Through investigation of literacy use and cultural practices, learners develop metacognitive awareness of variations in form and function while also developing their own proficiency. Looking at who uses which language for what purposes, how literacy develops, and attitudes towards bilingualism promotes critical reflection on schooling and education.

7. Content also comes from the immediate context of the classroom. Because the students' primary shared context is their learning community, negotiating classroom dynamics and procedures is an important part of the content. By transforming these issues into content-based literacy activities, involving students in examining student-teacher roles, making decisions about curriculum content and processes, and resolving conflict, roles and social relations in the classroom can be redefined.

8. Individual experience is linked to social analysis. Participants look at their personal situations in light of each others' experiences and examine the root causes of problematic conditions. Thus, they talk not only about someone's difficulties finding an apartment, but about why there is a housing shortage, about why some landlords prefer to rent to immigrants and others prefer not to, and about strategies for finding housing. This collective reflection depersonalizes problems, provides support, and is the basis for action.

9. The content goes back to the social context. The goal is action outside the classroom to address participants' concerns; content is meaningful to the extent that it enables learners to make changes in their lives. This means that reality is not seen as static or immutable; learners can do more than adapt to it. Thus, literacy is not the end in itself, but rather a means for participants to shape reality, accomplishing their own goals. Skills are taught in service of action for change rather than as independent, isolated objectives.

2 Getting Started: Program Structure

Now comes the hard part—making the leap from the ideal to reality. The previous chapter examined some of the theoretical underpinnings of a participatory approach, but there's always a tension between the real and the ideal. This was a tension we struggled with from the very beginning in our project. We had a clear idea of what we wanted to do in terms of drawing out students' issues, centering the curriculum around them, and making literacy more significant in their lives. But the first lesson we learned was that no classroom exists in a bubble: It's unrealistic to think that the way a participatory curriculum develops depends entirely on what happens once people have walked in the door. The issues, the content, and the dynamics inside a classroom are shaped before anyone ever enters it, by decisions that have been made outside it.

Your Practice...

Again, before proceeding, take some time to explore your own ideas about the relationship between structural and curricular issues. If you are setting up a program, respond to the following questions in terms of possible options: Discuss advantages and disadvantages of choices and their implications. If your program is already in progress, respond in terms of the existing structure and reactions you have to it. Why were choices made and what have their consequences been? What problems have arisen as a result of these choices?

1. The institutional context
♦ Who was involved in finding funding, designing the project, and writing the proposal?
♦ Does the project involve collaboration? If so, with whom?
♦ What are the values and expectations of the institutions involved?
♦ What are the mandates/constraints from funders that have shaped program design? Are you uncomfortable with any of these?
♦ How have you addressed or might you address these concerns?

2. Staffing
♦ What are the staff positions? Are staff part-time or full-time?
♦ How are staff selected? Who is involved in the selection process?
♦ What qualifications are required? Why?
♦ Are roles and responsibilities differentiated? If so, how?
♦ What is the teaching load? prep time? other?
♦ How/when does staff development take place? Who is involved?

3. Time
♦ How long does each teaching cycle last?
♦ How many hours per week of class time is there?
♦ What time of the day do classes take place?
♦ How many cycles can students participate in?
♦ Is enrollment open or limited to certain times?

4. Site/location
♦ Where is the program housed (e.g., school, library, housing project)?
♦ How does the location impact participation?

5. Learner population and recruitment
♦ What population has been targeted for participation (e.g., a single language group or a multilingual group; working people, unemployed people, or welfare recipients)?
♦ Do participants come from a single community?
♦ How and where does recruitment take place? Who is involved in it?
♦ How is the project presented (what is said about it)?

6. Intake
♦ Who is involved in placing students?
♦ How is it done? individually/group? interviews? testing? what kind?
♦ How is information from intake used? Who has access to this information?
♦ On what basis are placements made? level of ESL (oral/literacy)? level of first language literacy? interest? language group? other?
♦ Do students have any choices about placement?

7. Orientation
♦ How are students oriented to the program?
♦ What are students told when they enroll?

8. Support services
♦ What support services are available—childcare? counseling? job placement? transportation? other?
♦ How do different components of the program work together?

9. Other: Are there other structural factors that affect your practice?

Our Practice...   When we started our project, we did not realize the extent to which answers to the questions above would shape our curriculum development process. It was not until we were fully underway that we recognized the importance of a priori decisions about program structure in determining what we could or couldn't do in classes. Choices about how teachers were hired, how students were recruited, how the project was presented to students, and, most importantly, how all these decisions were made, influenced our work. Institutional factors—what funders expected, what else was going on at the sites, the norms and assumptions these institutional practices were embedded in—had a powerful effect on our practice. We quickly came to realize that it's not just the students' context that influences curriculum development; it's also the conditions that surround our own work. Often, our meeting time was taken by dealing with these issues rather than with purely instructional ones. Although at the time this seemed troublesome, in retrospect, it seems inevitable: Program structure and curriculum development cannot be separated. In other words, we need to add another guiding principle to the list at the end of Chapter 1: *The context of the project shapes the possibilities.*

There are several lessons to be learned from this experience. The first is that, ideally, the kinds of questions raised here should be addressed *before* a proposal for funding is submitted, because in most cases, the mandates of the proposal dictate practice; once the project is funded, you're pretty much bound to the design specified. While there are always conditions over which we have little control, there are also many points during the process of setting up programs where choices can be made that will have significant consequences for how the classes develop.

The second and most critical lesson is that decisions can best be made by those who will carry them out and be affected by them, namely, practitioners: *It is always necessary to build in time, money, and a process for collaborative decision-making among the staff.* Paid staff meeting time is the key to effective programming; it is absolutely essential and worth every penny of funding it takes.

Finally, there are no right or wrong answers to the questions at the beginning of this chapter. Since the essence of a participatory approach is that it is context-specific, it doesn't make sense to promote a single program model for any context here. Structural choices have to fit the circumstances of each program. What we can do, though, is examine some of the factors that need to be taken into account, present our experience in making choices about these factors, and discuss issues and implications that emerged from these choices. The following sections cover each of the factors listed in "Your Practice" in this way.

The Institutional Context

Project Administration

Before our project even began, a number of structural choices were made that shaped the way the project developed for the next three years. The original idea came from the university. Once faculty decided to pursue funding, a meeting was called with existing community-based adult literacy centers to invite collaboration. Three sites decided to work on the project. UMass faculty wrote the proposal with input from these groups. While there was dialogue at every point along the way, UMass served as the umbrella organization, receiving and distributing the funding, negotiating with funders, and administering the program. This choice was made because it was logistically simpler than having several institutions jointly receive funding; we felt it would enhance our chances for favorable consideration. The size of the university, its status as an institution of higher education, its history of administering grants, and the grant-writing experience and professional qualifications of faculty members were seen as advantages in terms of securing funding that could be used to enhance the work of grass roots agencies.

Issue: What is collaboration? Despite the fact that we called ourselves a collaborative project, we had to figure out what this really meant along the way. We had to negotiate questions such as the following: How are decisions about hiring teachers made? Whose agenda are we following? How should budget decisions be made? The community centers wondered at times if the locus of power was, in fact, in university hands, despite the university's protestations to the contrary, and if the university was truly committed to the students or mainly interested in pursuing research and publication goals. For their part, university staff wondered if the community centers were collaborating mainly in order to augment their own resources. Mutual trust had to be built over time because of the general history of divergent agendas of universities and community groups and because of the particular history of the project.

Implications. The nature of collaboration is shaped by initial encounters, the proposal writing process, the funding mechanisms, and administrative structures. If one group initiates the process and is formally identified as the umbrella organization, contacts with funders and logistical aspects of administration may be facilitated. However, if the collaboration is to be genuine, it is critical that this organization work actively to reflect the needs, build consensus, and ensure the involvement of each participating group in all decision-making. In any case, developing true collaboration is always a process that takes time and goes beyond formal agreements.

Dual Structure

In order to ensure the collaborative nature of our project, a dual structure was set up. The university secured and administered the grant; most of the implementation took place at the three program sites. Staff were selected jointly, but employed by the university. The teachers were based at the community centers, the coordinator at the university, and the curriculum specialist somewhere in between, linking the teachers to each other and to the project as a whole. Weekly staff meetings rotated among centers so that everyone would become familiar with each others' workplaces, and so that nonproject teachers from each site could come to open training sessions held at their site. In addition, project teachers participated in all the functions of their centers as regular staff members. To facilitate the integration of the project into ongoing community program activities and to ensure that the programs felt ownership of the project, we followed existing program procedures and structures in terms of hiring, student recruitment, placement, and scheduling as much as possible. As a result, certain structural features of the project (e.g., length and schedule of cycles, intake procedures, and in some cases, course load) varied from site to site.

Issue: Is the project an extension of ongoing work or an independent entity? The dual structure of the project seemed at times to be an advantage; it meant that the project was integrated organically into existing community-based literacy work. At other times, it was a challenge to balance the needs of the project and the needs of the sites, which were not always the same. Although we wanted to be sure that our work complemented what was already going on in each center, serving the real needs of the programs and the students, we also wanted to be sure that our work was innovative and had an independent character. Teachers, in particular, felt the brunt of this tension, trying to balance site and project responsibilities and allegiances and decide how to allocate their time and energy.

Implications. Communication is the key to integrating a new project with ongoing work. There must be clear lines of communication between administrators and teachers as well as among teachers. To facilitate this, *project teachers must be recognized as official voices of the project because they are the primary link between collaborating institutions.* They must be involved in staff meetings so that they understand the constraints and conditions at their sites. Further, site staff at all levels must be involved in dialogue about the rationale and implications of the project so that they don't feel that outsiders or administrators are making decisions that affect their work.

Funders' Constraints

For us, the issue of funders' constraints came up clearly around the question of who to enroll in classes and how to define course content in terms of family literacy issues. Although ESL family literacy programs are designed to target parents of bilingual children to enable them to support their children's literacy development, the concept of the nuclear family doesn't always fit the reality of immigrants' and refugees' living situations. In their own cultures, family units may include much wider circles of relationships. On the other hand, many refugee and immigrant families have been torn apart by war and migration. Children often have been left behind or live with unrelated caregivers. Even finding out about students' family situations can be a delicate process (given that family status is used to determine documentation, benefits, etc.). We decided to be as inclusive as possible in our definition of family, rather than limit classes to those who fit one culture-specific notion of family. This meant enrolling grandparents, aunts, uncles, and sometimes unrelated caregivers in our classes. Further, once classes began, we discovered that students wanted to address a host of issues extending beyond family literacy content (see facing page).

Issue: How can we balance students' needs with funders' mandates? For us, this dilemma took the following form: How can we call ourselves a family literacy project if we define family so broadly and include content that isn't specifically related to family literacy? If we limit family literacy classes to parents of language minority students, we miss important segments of the relevant population; but if we broaden our definition to correspond to the reality of these children's lives, we may be diluting the focus of the work (because of the broadened range of interests and issues of participants). This ceased to be a contradiction for us, however, when we saw that family literacy means more than narrow didactic encounters between parent and child. In our own project, when we grasped the concept that the essence of family literacy is making literacy socially significant in family life, we were able to stop worrying about not focusing enough on direct parent-child literacy work.

Implications. While it is difficult to generalize from the experience of one project, the key for us in figuring out how to reconcile funders' constraints with classroom realities was analyzing the conditions of students' lives and always trying to put their needs first. Our sense was that, even when constraints seemed insurmountable, there were openings for this kind of reconciliation through analysis and responsiveness to student needs.

Balancing Students' Needs With Funders' Mandates

The following passages are excerpts from the minutes of our teacher sharing meetings where we discussed this issue and its implications for the curriculum.

But how much should we talk about families anyway? For many students and teachers, family related issues are extremely loaded. Death, separation from loved ones and imprisonment are common realities for our students. It's hard for students to talk about these issues. This presents a dilemma for us. We're funded to address family literacy issues; but students may be uncomfortable about dealing with them, and we are a participatory project based on the premise that learning must start with issues that *students* want to talk about. Our role as teachers is to find students' issues rather than impose ones which we have selected. So how do we center the curriculum on *family* if that's not what students want to do?

Teachers addressed this dilemma in two ways. First, they stressed that one never knows, as a teacher, when loaded issues will arise in the course of classroom interaction. The most seemingly innocuous topic (food) can raise heavy issues for students. So, in a way, it's impossible to steer away from issues because they may be too threatening or personal for students. The other aspect of this is that we must avoid a narrow focus on family issues if we define family literacy issues as any issues which impact on the family literacy environment, including things like employment, child care, housing, etc. We need to intersperse family-centered content with catalysts for getting at other issues, and with lighter, more traditional activities.

Staffing

Hiring

The hiring process was done collaboratively; the sites did the preliminary selection of candidates and the project coordinator represented the university in the final interviews. Each site followed its own established process in hiring. In some cases, students were involved in the interviews; in some, candidates were asked to teach a class. At two sites, the entire teaching staff participated in the decision-making; at another, the decision was made by an administrator. At one site, the project coordinator raised reservations about the finalist because the candidate didn't meet the requirements specified in the proposal. The process had not been formalized so there was some misunderstanding about how the final decision-making would take place. At another site, where the hiring was done only by the administrator, there was sometimes a sense of distance between the project teacher and other teachers on the staff.

Issue: How can a participatory hiring process be ensured while at the same time respecting the varying procedures of sites and the mandates of the grant? On the one hand, it is clear that broadening the selection process to include teachers and students is very much in keeping with a participatory approach. It is educational and motivating for students to participate in discussion about teaching qualifications and increases the chances that the person selected will be an effective teacher. It is important for teachers to participate in selecting their colleagues, both because they have a realistic sense of the job requirements and because it gives them the opportunity to learn more about the project. At the same time, it would be intrusive to impose a participatory process at a site where it wasn't welcomed by staff; in addition, if the results of the participatory selection process differed from the funding mandates, a conflict could arise.

Implications. Guidelines for the hiring process should be clearly articulated as part of the initial negotiations between representatives of the collaborating programs and institutions. The rationale for student and teacher participation should be part of these discussions as should the rationale for qualifications specified by funders (this issue is discussed more fully on the following page). Wherever possible, involvement should be broad and participatory—so that hiring decisions are integrated into the instructional process.

Teacher Qualifications

Because proposals are often viewed more favorably if proposed project staff have higher formal qualifications, we specified in our proposal that all teachers hired would have an M.A. (as well as teaching experience). This created a contradiction, however. The success of a community-based literacy project depends largely on the teachers' ties to the communities of the learners; but because of the constraints in the proposal, we resisted hiring a candidate who had a wealth of teaching experience and excellent references, was from the community of the learners and was herself an ESL speaker, but who didn't have an M.A. However, subsequent experience confirmed that when teachers' life experiences are similar in some way to students', the class has additional resources to draw on and possibilities are expanded. Another teacher with a similar background was able to pursue new issues and directions in her class because she shared the students' language and culture and was herself a mother.

Issue: How do we weigh the importance of formal qualifications and informal qualifications (i.e., practical experience and ties to the communities of the learners)? On the one hand, because of the way proposals are evaluated, it is necessary to specify advanced degrees; on the other hand, the effectiveness of a teacher's work depends in large measure on an ability to relate to students and to engender trust. For this reason, nontraditional qualifications, such as shared experience, language, and cultural background, are particularly important. These conflicting demands, however, create a Catch-22: The reality is that, because very little specialized education or training in adult ESL/literacy is available and salaries are relatively low, it is difficult to find bilingual/bicultural candidates with relevant advanced degrees. Those with certification have been trained to work with children (training that is often irrelevant or unsuited for work with adults) and can find better paying jobs in elementary/secondary education. Those with relevant background and experience are often excluded because of a lack of formal credentials.

Implications. Although it would be advantageous to have staff with both advanced degrees and ties to the communities of the learners, this is not always possible. Thus, it is important not to exclude candidates with strong backgrounds solely on the basis of lack of formal credentials and to recognize ways of gaining knowledge other than formal education. As adult educators, we must advocate broadening the definition of qualifications to include practical experience and relevant cultural background; these informal qualifications should be recognized in proposal evaluations.

Roles and Responsibilities

Our project started with a three-way differentiation of roles. The project coordinator was responsible for training, disseminating information, overseeing the work of the project, and providing leadership. The curriculum specialist was responsible for coordinating curriculum development, working on special projects, and participating in information dissemination. The teachers' primary work was in the classroom, developing and implementing the curriculum.

Issue: How can a project be participatory with a differentiation of roles? A number of tensions arose from this role differentiation. Because the coordinator wasn't in the classroom, she sometimes came in with ideas about what teachers should be doing that didn't correspond to the realities of the classroom. Teachers insisted on determining the direction of their own classes, sometimes resisting the coordinator's primary role in shaping the content of training. To the extent that the coordinator was the main spokesperson for the project, teachers felt that their own voices weren't represented; at the same time, the coordinator felt divorced from the exciting work that was going on in the classrooms, and the curriculum specialist's role wasn't always clear given that a participatory approach is grounded in developing curriculum out of the particular context of a class. As a result, we went through a process of redefining roles, with teachers developing their own forms for staff development, becoming increasingly involved in dissemination, and establishing an independent voice in documentation. At the same time, however, teachers felt a tension between wanting to have a voice in all aspects of the work, but not having the time or inclination to do everything. We worked toward a sharing of decision-making and responsibilities with different staff members still focusing on certain areas.

Implications. Clear-cut divisions in responsibility may impose hierarchical relationships and create a separation between theory and practice, particularly if the coordinator has special status as an expert, divorced from the reality of the classroom, but in a position to influence its direction. If the essence of a participatory approach is context-specific learning, it's a contradiction to separate practitioners' work from curriculum development or training. On the other hand, it's neither efficient nor possible for everyone to do everything. What makes sense is a nonhierarchical structure where participants' work overlaps (but doesn't require everyone to do everything), decisions are made together, and expertise is developed collaboratively.

Teacher Workload

Teachers in our project were full-time employees with benefits including medical insurance and paid vacation time. Each teacher taught two levels of classes, and in some cases opted to teach additional elective courses. Their other responsibilities included curriculum development, information dissemination, training, participation in site and project meetings, and other site responsibilities (e.g., intake, assessment, evaluation). Paid time for preparation, professional development, and nonteaching activities was probably the single most important factor in their ability to be effective as teachers, to develop innovative curricula, and to contribute to the the field of adult ESL literacy.

Issue: How can programs balance the need to be cost-effective with the need for quality teaching? In order to get funding, programs need to serve as many people as possible, for as little money as possible; consequently, teachers are often hired on a part-time basis or given heavy course loads. Further, the salary range in adult education is considerably lower than it is in other sectors of public education. The result is that teachers often run from job to job, burn out quickly, have no time for innovation, and leave the field after a few years. When we met other family literacy teachers at conferences, they often told us that they taught a few classes at night in addition to other jobs, and had little time to prepare or even think about curriculum issues. Their family literacy classes were often no different from other ESL classes. They rarely met with colleagues to discuss common concerns or share teaching strategies. In our case, it was precisely because teachers had paid time to read, write, and talk about their work that they were able to be effective inside the classroom and contribute to the development of the field.

Implications. The choice between quality full-time teaching and cost-effectiveness is a false choice. In order for instruction to be effective and for the field of adult literacy to develop, teachers must be treated as professionals, and supported in terms of salary, working conditions, and intellectual development. It is the teachers who ultimately determine the quality of adult literacy and it is only when they are recognized, given paid time to meet with each other, to reflect on and document their practice, that the delivery of services will improve and the field as a whole will move forward. Teaching cannot be divorced from professional development.

Staff Development

Our project started with a traditional training model in which the coordinator was responsible for selecting topics, designing the syllabus and conducting the trainings. As coordinator, I came to early staff meetings with a plan for each session, and began by presenting information, suggesting readings and trying to lead discussions. It soon became clear that this wasn't working: Teachers felt that the readings had little relation to the realities of their classrooms.

Issue: How can training address the tension between expanding teachers' knowledge base and responding to practical issues and classroom realities? While I was trying to create a theoretical and conceptual framework for the project, teachers were immersed in issues such as "How can I find out what students are interested in if we don't share a common language?" They needed time to talk about issues arising from their practice, and for this, they were each others' best resources. My input was valid but no more important than theirs. In other words, the training needed to be driven by the teachers' practice, rather than their practice driven by the training. Nevertheless, I was concerned that they weren't getting the information they needed from the knowledge base of research and professional literature to which I had access. I continued to suggest readings or topics. Very often, when it came time to discuss them, the teachers, (like Rosa, a student, p. 8) hadn't done their homework. But, like Rosa, when the homework emerged out of one of *their* concerns, and they felt a need for a particular kind of external resource, they became engaged. In other words, when their learning was self-directed, arising out of their own needs, it was most useful. I had to let go of the idea that, I, as the trainer, was responsible for shaping their learning based on what *I* thought was important, and to stop feeling guilty if we deviated from the agenda. The model we arrived at drew on both our own and outside resources. Its central component was teacher-sharing (described in Chapter 3 as the core of curriculum development). We also had workshops on a variety of topics chosen by the teachers.

Implications. Staff development, like teaching, is most effective when it is participatory. It needs to be ongoing and contextualized, emerging out of the real issues and questions teachers are facing. This means redefining expertise so that teachers' experience and role in constructing knowledge count. We need to move toward an "everyone teaches, everyone learns" model with each other as well as in our work with students.

Time: Length of Cycles and Duration of Classes

Length of cycles and duration of classes were determined on a site-by-site basis. There were three cycles per year of about twelve weeks each, with four to twelve hours per week of instructional time for each student. Working students preferred night classes that met four hours a week; for nonworking students with school-age children, daytime classes with several hours of instruction per day seemed better. Of course, classes that met most often were better able to develop the participatory process; the momentum around an issue can be lost if there is too much time between classes. Some students stayed in a family literacy class for one cycle before moving on; others stayed for up to two years. Because levels of English proficiency were low, it took time to develop students' proficiency to the point where they could go on to higher level classes. In addition, they often didn't want to leave the class because it provided a supportive context for learning, focused on issues that were meaningful to them, and developed their sense of self-confidence. At the same time, however, there were long waiting lists of students in need of classes.

Issue: How can we both serve the growing number of students and provide adequate learning time and continuity of instruction? Although initial literacy acquisition takes years for children, it is often expected that nonliterate adults will acquire similar levels of competence (in a second language!) in a fraction of the time. The rate of progress depends to a large extent on the student's starting point. Yet, in the interests of efficiency and access, funders limit the time that students can stay in programs, favor projects that claim to achieve the biggest gains in the shortest time, and make funding contingent on mandated levels of progress. As a result, the least literate students are either excluded altogether because it takes longer to show progress, or they are cycled out quickly to increase the number of students served. This has the effect of maintaining the low level of the least literate students.

Implications. Beyond advocating for more funding to accommodate the growing number of students, we need to challenge the notion that it is always better for students to exit from classes as quickly as possible. Rather, we need to provide a range of time options for students that take into account work and family schedules as well as educational needs. Decisions about timing should be left to the judgement of educators, rather than mandated by funders.

Should We Give Students as Much Time as Possible, or Move Them Along as Quickly as We Can?

The following passages are excerpts from the minutes of our project staff meetings where we discussed this issue and its implications for the students.

Teachers were concerned about numbers. Will we have to cycle students out of our classes as quickly as possible to meet the 150 students per year goal? What if some students need more time? Teachers were concerned that, given the student population (with very low skill levels), there be a conscious policy of retaining students as long as necessary to really show progress. Since this project is one of the few that meets the very real need of serving students who are far from being employable or moving to GED (in a state climate of funding only employment-related ESL), it is important that we not try to move students through quickly, but rather, keep them long enough to ensure substantial progress. There is a trade-off: Numbers may be lower, but the quality and effectiveness of instruction will be enhanced.

Charo now has almost all new students in her upper level class because everyone else went on to a higher level; one even went to level 3. She feels mixed about this because it means that the support community for the students is disrupted; there's a certain way of doing things and sense of community which was established that helped students in her class learn and she has mixed feelings about letting go of this. Madeline also talked about this dilemma of feeling the students need to maintain their learning community but also need to progress to other levels.

Site/Location

Most of our classes were at adult learning centers, one was in a public housing project, one was in an apartment complex, and one was in a library. No classes were held in public schools because of our concern about participants' possible negative associations with schools. (Another family literacy program in the Boston area had done recruitment through the schools and met with some resistance.) There were two criteria for selecting locations: convenience for students and impact on participation. We found that the place a class meets influences who participates and how the curriculum develops. For example, although availability of space was the main reason for meeting in the library, that class was able to develop familiarity with library use and resources in a way that others couldn't. When one of our teachers started a class in a Hispanic apartment complex, students with literacy levels much lower than those who came to the center for classes began to participate because the site itself was familiar and less intimidating than a learning center.

Issue: Should students come to us, or should we go to them? It is often more convenient for staff to centralize classes in one location; it facilitates logistics (such as xeroxing), and means teachers don't have to travel around transporting books and materials. However, in adult literacy, *turf* is a critical issue for students, partly because of transportation (cost, distance, time, etc.), partly because of effort (it's harder for students to mobilize themselves to do something difficult if they have to travel to an alien place), but mostly because of familiarity and comfort. Students with little prior education often feel like strangers in school settings. If they are on their own turf, there is one less reason for apprehension about learning. In addition, issues of importance will emerge more readily in an atmosphere where students feel a sense of ownership. Since content comes from the social context in a participatory approach, it is easier to find common issues if the students come from and work in an immediate shared context; issues relating to the community of the housing project are more likely to become course content if classes take place there.

Implications. There is a strong connection between where classes are located, who will come, and how curriculum will develop. It is critical to become familiar enough with the learners' community to know the significance of different places in their lives. This means being willing to be flexible and, if necessary, to move the location as you learn more about the community. *Sometimes you have to go to students instead of expecting them to come to you.*

Learner Populations

Heterogeneous vs. Homogeneous Groupings

We decided early in our project that we would take students as they came, attempting to meet their needs, rather than establish rigid entry criteria to simplify our work, ensure monolithic classes, and facilitate implementation. In some cases, this meant that classes were multilingual, while in others, students came from a single language group. Some classes had only mothers or women, while others were mixed. In some, literacy levels were quite varied, while in others they were similar. Class make-up was influenced by how recruitment was done and where classes were held.

Issue: How do we balance the benefits of homogeneous vs. diverse classes? In our experience, diversity among students had several advantages: Students had a real need to use English to communicate with each other; there was peer learning and a lively exchange of perspectives; and the range of issues was broad. Students were often amazed and moved by each others' histories, which allowed them to see their own experiences in a new light. At the same time, however, diversity imposed limitations, making it difficult to meet individual needs and find themes that everyone wanted to pursue. In one class, students of different nationalities, ages, and educational backgrounds worked together for two years exploring this diversity as a strength, and then chose to go in different directions to meet individual needs. In single language classes, it was easier to identify common issues, and to build on first language literacy skills; however, it sometimes was difficult to sustain use of English. Classes with women only seemed more open, with a greater sense of ease in raising issues from participants' lives.

Implications. There is a richness in diversity that allows students to see their own experience in a broader perspective, learn from each other and use language as a bridge between cultures. At the same time, however, too much diversity can be counterproductive, impeding the participatory process. Since participatory education aims to link what happens inside class to action for change outside class, it is important that students share a context in which to take action. If students come from the same housing project, language background, workplace, or neighborhood, if they are all women or all mothers, if their children are similar in age or go to the same school, it will be easier to find common issues and to develop an organizational basis for acting on them. It matters less *what* the unifying framework is than that there be one.

What Are the Advantages and Disadvantages of Homogeneous Grouping?

The following passages are excerpts from the minutes of our project staff meetings where we discussed this issue and its implications for the students.

Alicia used Ann's interview lesson about life journeys with two of her classes. What struck her was the answers from the lower group were more interesting. This group is composed of different nationalities so there seemed to be more of an exchange of information.

Charo has a class that's all women. The group dynamics are completely different. People seem more relaxed and open. Issues are coming out more easily and there's a lot more laughter.

Loren's class is focusing on school-related work, examining students' own educational background and views about schooling. As the link is made with children's education, what seems to be emerging is an interest in teenagers issues: dealing with drugs, sex, etc. rather than reading with kids; what's appropriate for this group is different than what would be appropriate for parents of younger children. They seem to be more interested in dealing with parent-child issues as the content for their own literacy activities rather than family literacy processes (like doing literacy activities with kids).

In Charo's mothers and children class, the mothers have begun to spontaneously read to kids and work alongside them. Each class starts with a ritual of interacting with the kids. When the parents start doing their own work, very often the kids ask for the work their parents are doing. Even the little kids scribble on worksheets their parents are doing—and the scribbles are in the right places, on the lines. Charo feels that this model of not separating childcare from the classroom is beneficial for the whole family—learning becomes fun for the children and a connection between parent and child.

Recruitment

How students are recruited and what they are told about the project will influence curriculum development. An informal survey at one of the sites indicated that most students hear about programs by word of mouth rather than through formal publicity; they come because someone they trust told them about it, not because they saw a flyer. Since the literacy centers in our project usually had long waiting lists, we did not do special recruitment for family literacy classes, but selected appropriate students from existing lists; participants often did not know they were part of a special project and did not explicitly choose to participate. However, in some cases, special outreach was necessary: One teacher discovered a group of students who came to her site for social services but didn't sign up for ESL because they were illiterate in Spanish and were intimidated by the idea of school; thus, there was a built-in referral connection right at the site that hadn't been tapped. Another center decided to offer an additional family literacy class, publicizing it as a class for parents interested in helping their children with reading and homework; but too few people signed up and the class was cancelled.

Issue: Should recruitment be general or targeted? Any project with a special focus (like our family literacy project) needs to consider the advantages and disadvantages of targeting recruitment to a particular group of students. The disadvantage of nontargeted recruitment is that students may not see the classes as any different from general ESL classes, making it difficult to focus on issues specific to the project focus. At the same time, however, adults may not want to come to classes that focus only on a single topic: They may have a broader range of interests. (This may be why the class for parents never got off the ground: Its focus was too narrow.) This issue is not specific to family literacy. Many teachers in workplace programs, for example, say that their students don't always want to work on work-related issues; they are whole people who have concerns that extend beyond employment.

Implications. A balance needs to be struck between making the course topic explicit and not limiting classes to that focus. To do this, there needs to be both targeted recruitment and some self-selection by students. Advertising a topic-specific class may not attract students; personal (bilingual) contact is important. Once potential participants have been identified, they should be given the option of joining a topic-related class, and information on which to base their choice. For example, since the term "family literacy" may be unfamiliar, students should be asked if they would like to join a class that focuses primarily on their concerns about their children's reading, schoolwork, and schooling, but also on other issues of concern to them.

Intake

Since intake was done according to the procedures of each center in our project, we were able to compare different models. The sites varied in terms of why intake was done (rationale), what it consisted of (content), how it was done (process/tone), and who did it. In one site, intake was done by counselors who got information about students' life situations, did a formal assessment, and passed test scores on to an administrator who used them for placement. Results were shared neither with students nor teachers. About one fourth of the students were inappropriately placed, assessment was divorced from instruction, and the intake did not reflect the program's pedagogical approach. At another site, intake was done by teachers using an informal interview process. A range of factors was considered for placement, including literacy level, interests, and group cohesiveness. Teachers shared information from the intake process with each other so it could be used to inform curriculum development.

Issue: How can intake be both participatory and efficient? Very often, in the interests of streamlining placements, intake is done according to the first of the above models. While the initial process may be facilitated, long-term consequences may be negative. Intake is the students' critical first encounter with a program. It sends them messages about themselves, about what education is, and about what literacy is. For low-level students, testing can be a threatening ordeal that reinforces feelings of inadequacy. Not sharing test results with them makes them objects of an alien process, reinforcing a sense of powerlessness. Tests that emphasize matching sounds to symbols, reading word lists or street signs, or filling out forms, convey the message that literacy is a set of skills, either decontextualized or limited to functional purposes (rather than a way to make sense of or change one's life). On the other hand, if intake allows students to show what they know, express their interests, and begin to explore their own literacy uses and purposes, they get a sense of directing their own learning. Teachers are in the best position to carry out this type of interview efficiently, without it being too cumbersome or time-consuming, since they can interpret subjective information in interviews.

Implications. Teachers should be involved in developing and carrying out intake because they are best able to link intake procedures to a learner-centered pedagogy, interpret and share results, place students in appropriate classes, and utilize information to inform curriculum development. (Specific guidelines and procedures for intake are presented in Chapter 8.)

Orientation

We had the opportunity to compare approaches to orientation as one site experimented with two different models during the course of the project. In the first model, the director welcomed students at the beginning of each cycle and presented information about services. A counselor then presented the attendance policy, specifying how many absences were permitted before students would be dropped. Teachers were introduced and greeted students briefly. As one teacher said, students were "talked at and the speeches amounted to 45 minutes of threats." The result was that students were made to feel like children whose situations, problems, and concerns would not be taken into account. No one who went to one of these orientations ever returned for another.

Issue: How can orientation set the tone for instruction? The new model at the same site is much more informal and interactive. Orientation starts with music and refreshments. After a brief welcome, each teacher presents something about the program in Spanish, even if it means struggling and making mistakes in front of the group. The message this sends is that it's okay to struggle in a second language and that everyone is both learning and teaching. Seeing teachers in this light puts students at ease and introduces the pedagogical approach. Further, even though the attendance policy is articulated, teachers also acknowledge students' situations and difficulties in coming to class. This is followed by a small-group activity where students get to know each other (including people who may not be in their classes). Once this model was introduced, students began coming back to orientation at the beginning of each cycle. The orientation is like a social event that they want to participate in. In fact, people who have not been admitted come as well; they've heard that the center is a good place and come to orientation as a way to check it out. In addition, retention has turned around; perhaps in part because their outside problems are seen as valid, students come to class more often.

Implications. Orientation, like intake, sets the tone for the whole educational endeavor. These initial encounters convey a message about what the center is like, how students will be treated, and what education is. If students are treated like children, and information is conveyed in a transmission mode, they don't feel a sense of ownership and ease. They feel like they are on alien turf. Thus, the same principles that guide participatory classroom interaction need to guide orientation and intake: Students need to be treated as equals and given the opportunity to begin building a learning community. This kind of participatory atmosphere has consequences for classroom dynamics, enrollment, and retention.

Support Services

One of our sites had a full range of support services: childcare, counseling, legal assistance, job placement, and housing assistance. Another developed a community support program in which students were hired and trained in different areas (e.g., housing, immigration law) so they could assist other students. These two models allowed us to see the benefits and pitfalls of different support structures. In the program with more services, the support component was structurally separate from the instructional component. There was little communication among counselors, day care workers, and teachers. The underlying assumption seemed to be that students were needy victims who had to be helped in solving problems; their problems were treated as external obstacles to be taken care of by experts. In the site with the community assistance program, students were trained as experts in particular areas so that they could become resources for their peers. In addition, class time was devoted to addressing support issues through curriculum content.

Issue: How can programs balance the need for support services with the need to develop students' capacity to address their own problems? Although clearly students benefit from having as many support resources as possible to facilitate their participation, we found that the way services are presented can foster either reliance on others for assistance or self-reliance. When problems are marginalized from the classroom, treated as individual issues, and handed over to outside experts, the cycle of dependency is reinforced. To the extent that teachers become social workers, trying to solve students' problems for them, they themselves become overwhelmed and undermine students' ability to address problems using their own resources. On the other hand, when problems are brought into the classroom and addressed collectively, curriculum content can become the basis for action, which is the essence of a problem-posing approach.

Implications. While support services are important for effective adult education, the way they are integrated into programs is critical. The guiding principle—that students must be involved in a participatory, problem-posing way—applies here as well as in curriculum development. This means that support and instructional components must be closely linked and problems dealt with through both contexts. Structures for developing students' expertise and capacity to address their own problems must be set up wherever possible.

Support: Dependency or Self-Reliance?

The following passages are excerpts from the minutes of our project staff meetings where we discussed this issue and its implications for the students.

[A teacher] has recently discovered a built-in connection for recruiting students who are not literate right at her site. There are many people who come to the center for social services (legal/housing assistance etc.) who don't read and write in Spanish—they sign their names with an X. These are people who don't sign up for ESL but are already part of the center's population and could easily be referred to classes by counselors. The fact that this connection is only now being discovered reflects the separation of the educational and the social service components at sites...

In a discussion about how the educational philosophy of programs affects classroom possibilities, teachers said problems are often treated on an individual basis. Specifically, we talked about how attendance is often seen as a personal issue and dealt with through a counseling mode, which has the effect of removing it from the context of class/group discussion. In this way, the problems may disappear by being taken out of the teacher's hands but never really get addressed. We talked about how we can move from seeing things as personal to becoming part of the group responsibility.

The following examples show how issues traditionally seen as support issues can become part of curriculum content and the basis for action.

In Ann's center, there was a tension between the school where the program is housed and the program itself because children aren't supposed to be in the classrooms (but parents can't come if they don't bring their children). The teachers brought this issue to their students in a variety of ways. Ann devoted a class to the problem and her students decided to take a collection to hire a babysitter who could watch the kids in the pre-school space during class time.

Students in Charo's class have been talking about the problems of newcomers to Boston and all the things they have to deal with when they first arrive: finding a place to live, finding work, getting food, etc. They have decided to set up a bulletin board where students can post information about apartments which have space for someone to live, job openings, and free food programs.

The Practitioners' Bill of Rights

What practitioners need from funders and program administrators to provide effective (and therefore cost-effective) adult literacy/ESL instruction:

1. Full-time employment. Teachers must be hired fulltime so that they don't have to piece together several part-time jobs and can develop their work as professionals.

2. Competitive salary and benefits. Adult education teachers must be paid salaries comparable to other teachers and have benefits so that qualified people stay in the field and develop it.

3. Redefinition of qualifications. Nonformal education, linguistic and cultural background factors, teaching experience, and community ties should be given as much weight as formal education and advanced degrees in proposal evaluation and hiring.

4. Staff development time. Teachers must have paid time for training, teacher sharing, preparation, and curriculum development. Job descriptions and course loads should reflect these responsiblities.

5. Adequate instructional time for students. Teachers must have the ability to determine duration of instructional cycles and student progress with no unrealistic expectations for how long it takes to acquire ESL/literacy and no externally imposed limitations on length of instruction.

6. Autonomy. Teachers must be given autonomy in determining appropriate instructional content for their students rather than have curriculum and outcomes dictated by external needs.

7. Alternative evaluation. Programs should be evaluated through a variety of means (primarily qualitative) that reflect curriculum content, rather than solely on the basis of quantitative measures (test scores, grade levels, placements, etc.). Refunding should be contingent on a range of factors rather than on numbers alone.

8. Support services. Programming should include counseling, child care, and other support services. Communication between support and instructional components should be facilitated.

9. Participation in program management. Teachers should be involved in decision-making in all areas that affect their work (including intake, hiring, placement, and evaluation).

3 Into the Classroom: Overview of the Process and Ways of Finding Student Themes

In Chapter 1, we presented a theoretical framework for participatory curriculum development, outlining the rationale for this approach and the guiding principles for implementation. Chapter 2 began to address some of the hard realities of putting this approach into practice—how structural factors outside the classroom shape possibilities inside the classroom. In this chapter, we'll walk in the door of the classroom and begin to look at how a participatory cycle plays itself out with students. We'll present (a) a concrete overview of the steps of building a curriculum around student themes and (b) specific ways to begin this process by identifying student themes.

Your Practice...

Take a few minutes to describe and discuss a lesson or unit that you have recently completed or are in the middle of working on. If you're part of a group, talk about the lesson with your coworkers; if not, write up your account in a journal format.

1. Describe how you got into the unit/cycle.
♦ What was the theme or content of the lesson?
♦ Where did it come from? How did the theme emerge?
♦ What did you want to accomplish in the lesson? What were your hopes and expectations?

2. Describe what happened as the lesson developed.
♦ What activities did you use to develop the theme?
♦ What was the discussion surrounding the theme? How did students react? What did they say?
♦ What language skills were developed during this lesson?
♦ What new student issues or concerns emerged?

3. Share some of your reflections on what happened.
♦ How did the lesson differ from your expectations?
♦ What were some issues and concerns that arose for you as a teacher while doing this lesson?
♦ How might you follow up on this lesson?

Our Practice...

Teachers in our project talked about their practice every week using questions similar to those above to guide discussion. In the following excerpt from *Talking Shop: A Curriculum Sourcebook for Participatory Adult ESL*, (Nash, Cason, Rhum, McGrail & Gomez-Sanford, in press) Madeline describes how a unit unfolded in one of her classes.

> An example of using a student's concern as the content for a literacy lesson occurred when a student brought a traffic ticket that he did not understand to class. He told the class about the tickets he had gotten recently. One of them was a parking ticket; the other, a moving violation. It was the latter of the two that confused him. He brought the ticket to class because he wanted to pay it but did not know how to do so. I looked at the ticket and was not sure either. The extremely small print on the back of the ticket that is intended to explain the process for payment was written in legalese and was of no help. Other members of the class asked him about the circumstances in which he got the ticket. As it turned out, he was not sure what he had done wrong and when he asked the police officer to explain the

problem to him, he was ignored. We looked at the ticket, and the reason for issuing the ticket was not at all clear. As people asked more questions, he supplied more details about the incident, and about what he thought the reasons were for his receiving the ticket. Other students talked about the times they or their friends had gotten tickets. Several important issues emerged from this discussion: (a) racial discrimination; (b) illiteracy; (c) the difficulties of having limited English ability; and (d) quotas for ticketing.

For the following class, I wrote up the traffic ticket discussion as a reading. This generated further discussion about problems people had in dealing with the police. After several minutes, I suggested to the class that we could write a letter to the police commissioner or to the newspapers about these problems. Everyone thought this was a good idea. We talked about who to send it to and the students decided that the newspaper would be best because many people would read it and gain some understanding of the problems facing immigrants. We spent part of the class writing a language experience story in order to generate ideas about why we wanted to write this letter and what we wanted to say.

The next day, two members of the class who had been absent earlier in the week returned and objected to the letter writing. They felt that the letter accused the police of discrimination and that such a thing didn't exist except with a very few ignorant individuals. Some of the others felt strongly that there were problems of discrimination, particularly in Boston. After a rather heated discussion, everyone agreed to participate in the writing of the letter. The dissenters' decision to join the group may have been an indication of their desire to support their classmate rather than an acknowledgement of the existence of discrimination on a societal level.

We reviewed the LEA from the previous day, then continued writing down people's ideas. This time I tried to direct their comments by asking leading questions, such as: "What was wrong with the way the police officer was with Gebre?" and "What do you think the police should do in situations like this?"

Because the LEAs from the two days were not in any kind of logical order, the next step was to organize them. I wanted to be very careful at this point to help the students write a strong letter without imposing my idea of form and structure onto their work. For the next class, I wrote each sentence on a separate strip of newsprint. I introduced three categories into which the students were to put the sentences: (a) This is the problem; (b) Why we have this problem; and (c) Change (fix) the problem. The students read each sentence and decided together whether it belonged in category one, two, or three. After all the sentences were placed, we reread them and edited out the repetitions, and added an introduction and a closing.

It was very exciting for me to see the students collaborating on this critical thinking and editorial process. The better readers could read the sentences, and everyone, reader and nonreader alike, could participate in making the decisions about where each sentence sounded best and made the most sense. After they finished the editing process, I numbered each strip so I could remember the order and type up the letter.

I brought the typed letter to the class the next day. Everyone was proud of their work. Some people, however, were afraid to sign the letter because of feared recriminations. We talked about their fears and about the different ways police behave in different countries. In the end, people were reassured about the safety of publicly voicing this kind of complaint, and everyone signed the letter. (pp. 21-22)

In Madeline's class, the sequence of activities mirrored the steps of Freire's critical thinking process in a general way (from describing a problem, to analyzing its causes, to seeking solutions). She started by identifying a theme that came from a student's life. Because she was listening for issues, Madeline realized that the parking ticket question was relevant for the whole group and didn't try to answer the question on an individual basis as a teacher with a problem-solving outlook might have. She posed the problem to the whole group, facilitating discussion about its varying aspects and its causes.

At this point, she introduced a literacy activity, writing up the discussion in story form; this teacher-written text became the basis for reading work and further discussion. Dialogue on the second day linked the particular problem to the range of participants' experiences, putting it in a broader context. Madeline then made some suggestions for acting on the problem. This led to another literacy activity, a collaborative writing effort in which Madeline wrote the students' words using the language experience approach. The next day, discussion moved to a deeper level—that of societal discrimination. While no unanimous conclusion was reached, there was vigorous debate and critical thinking about an issue that touches students deeply. The process of group or collective action continued with the letter writing.

Madeline then introduced another literacy activity, moving to the level of composing: She provided a means for students to organize ideas even though their writing skills were weak. By providing mechanical support—writing the sentences on strips and cutting up the strips—she facilitated the process of moving to a higher conceptual level. In a sense, students were able to do a kind of manual word-processing using the strips. This method allowed these so-called low-level students to proceed to higher level skills: developing their ideas, organizing them, revising them, and editing them. The final outcome was an action that took the form of a letter.

On the next page is a schematic overview of the participatory curriculum process. In this book, Chapter 4 looks at the listening phase; Chapter 5 looks at tools for dialogue and literacy development; Chapter 6 looks at issues that arise in implementing these two components; and Chapters 7 and 8 look at action and evaluation.

This overview should be seen more as a hypothesis than a lock-step guide—something to be kept in mind but not rigidly adhered to. Schematizing in this way serves the important function of providing a conceptual overview to guide practice, but it doesn't capture the dynamic nature of how the process plays itself out in the classroom. *Talking Shop* (Nash et al., in press) presents accounts of what actually happens when these components are synthesized into classroom cycles.

While the overview below represents in schematic form the various components of a participatory process, it is important to remember that the way it plays itself out in practice changes every time around. Madeline's class differs from an idealized model in several ways: The issue involved didn't come as the result of an extended research phase; literacy activities were interspersed throughout, with a constant back and forth between analysis and reading/writing work, rather than a linear listening-dialogue-literacy work-action movement; the idea for action came from the teacher rather than from the group; the action didn't have any direct, overt impact on the outside world or on the conditions in students' lives. Finally, evaluation was not a separate, explicit stage.

Our experience has been that Madeline's class was typical in that it didn't follow the model exactly. An early misconception we had (based on taking Freire's work too literally) was that the components of the participatory process occur in a sequential order, starting with an extended period of identifying issues, developing a core set of units around these issues, and in each unit, moving systematically through structured dialogue, participatory classroom activities, actions outside the classroom, and group evaluation. However, the reality of adult ESL doesn't usually allow for a preliminary investigation stage in the students' community before classes begin, because students come from different backgrounds, language groups, parts of the city, and occupations. The classroom itself may be the only community that students have in common. Teachers, usually underpaid and parttime, are often too busy with other jobs to have time for outside investigation. In addition, we have found that issues never exist in a vacuum; they are situated in time and have power to the extent that they emerge from a particular situation. Madeline, for example, could not have decided before classes began that she wanted to work on police discrimination;

the unit worked because it came from a concrete situation. Hence, the identification of themes often emerges as a result of classroom interaction rather than as a precondition to it. Investigating student issues is a constant, ongoing, cyclical process, integrated into instruction. In practice, we often skip stages or jump back and forth between them. Many issues that teachers think are rich in potential end up wilting on the vine and never get beyond the dialogue phase. It's misleading to evaluate individual lessons in isolation, even though they may appear quite traditional. It is the progression of lessons in which students are increasingly involved that builds a participatory atmosphere.

Thus, we moved toward an understanding that themes and units didn't come in neat packages with beginnings, middles, and ends. More realistic than a sequence of extended phases (proceeding from investigation to dialogue, literacy, and action) is the notion of a series of short-term cycles, each of which starts with the emergence of a theme that is immediately explored through dialogue and sometimes followed by action and evaluation. As in Madeline's example, the literacy activities are woven throughout each cycle, coming at various points along the way. *The participatory nature of the class emerges through a cumulative process, rather than by following a sequential or linear procedure.*

Overview of
the Participatory Curriculum Development Process

Ways in: Listening to find student themes
During this phase, students and teachers work together to identify key/ loaded issues, themes, and concerns from the students' lives through:
- conscious listening before, during, and after class
- structured activities to elicit student themes (readings, grammar work, journals, responding to and producing drawings or photos, student research activities, interviews, language experience stories)

Tools: Dialogue and literacy development around themes
During this phase, student themes are explored using participatory tools to facilitate dialogue and literacy/language development. Tools include:
- published reading selections (from texts, newspapers, literature)
- teacher-written selections (short passages, codes—texts that represent problem situations)
- collaborative student-teacher texts (language experience stories, collaborative stories, dialogue journals)
- group and individual student writing (journals, letters, testimonials)
- oral histories
- photo stories

Action inside and outside the classroom
- Inside, students make changes in classroom dynamics, produce materials for use by others, participate in curriculum choices, and support each other in addressing problems in the process of doing literacy work.
- Outside, students participate in actions at the literacy center, in their families, workplaces and communities

Evaluation of learning and action
Students participate in evaluating their own progress, their actions, the teaching and the program as a whole; they reflect on outcomes and new issues which emerge from the process.

---

4 Ways In: Finding Student Themes

Whereas a more traditional approach starts with a priori needs assessments and curriculum outlines, a participatory approach starts by involving students in the process of uncovering themes and issues as an integral part of classroom interaction. This is what we call finding "ways in" to what's important to students (the listening component of the process).

Your Practice...

1. Describe a lesson or class from your experience in which students were particularly open and engaged with the topic.
♦ Where did the theme come from?
♦ Was it your idea? If so, why did you choose it?
♦ What led up to it—a structured activity? an overheard conversation?

2. List a few concerns or issues you think are important for your students.
♦ What happened to make you think they are important?

3. Describe a critical incident from your class—a time someone came to class with a problem, a story, a preoccupation; when students suddenly started talking in their native language; when someone missed class because of something important in their life; when there was an argument, tears, or laughter.
♦ How did the underlying issue embedded in the incident relate to others in the class?

4. Describe something unexpected that happened in one of your classes:
♦ Did you ever expect a certain response from students, but get a completely different one?
♦ Did something come up in class that made you throw out your lesson plans completely and "go with the flow?"

Our Practice...

Ideally, the kind of participant-observation in the community of the learners described by Freire is a powerful way to get to know the conditions and issues most critical for a particular group. However, as we said in Chapter 1, this approach may be neither practical nor effective for adult ESL in a North American context: Students often don't come from a single community, teachers don't have time to do this kind of intense participant observation, and most importantly, issues identified in this way lose some of their timeliness because they don't emerge from the actual, concrete concerns of participants. Although the teachers in our project had close ties to the communities of the learners and a general familiarity with issues of concern to them, the most powerful issues were often the ones that students themselves brought in or identified during the course of classroom interaction. Thus, classes went back and forth between themes identified by teachers based on their knowledge of the communities and issues that arose from the particular group.

Themes cannot be identified just by asking students what they want to study or what their concerns are. If students have internalized the very model of education that excluded them in the past—the teacher-fronted transmission-of-knowledge-and skills model—these questions may seem odd to them: Teachers are supposed to know what to do. Or, while they may appreciate being asked, students' answers may not be very productive. They may come up with vague goals (speaking better, improving English to get a better job, learning grammar, etc.) and the kinds of activities they are most familiar with (e.g., dictation, tests, workbook exercises). Finally, students may be suspicious of any questions that seem intrusive or personal. They are sometimes used to dealing with bureaucracies where information can be used against them. Without a basis of trust, they may be reluctant to share anything specific about their lives.

This means that the teacher's job at the beginning of each cycle is to set the tone, creating contexts for issues to emerge. The starting point has to be the building of trust through non-threatening activities that allow students to share something of their lives in a format that is familiar and comfortable. The first lesson for students has to be that their experiences are valued in the classroom and that it's safe to share parts of their lives with others.

Even when trust is built, however, it is important not to assume that issues will fall from the sky. Again, there must be a delicate balance between spontaniety and planning. Although it is clearly true that the most powerful issues emerge when we least expect them and have done nothing to find them, it is also true that we can't just sit around and wait for them to appear. We have to create the conditions for issues to emerge spontaneously and, at the same time, make a conscious effort to elicit them through structured, teacher-initiated activities. This means combining what we call *conscious listening* (an openness to going with the flow, hearing what's hidden between the lines, following up on diversions, etc.) with *catalyst activities* (guided language activities that encourage students to contribute their ideas, experiences and problems). Catalyst activities serve the dual purpose of providing the structured language lessons that students expect and triggering discussion which leads to the identification of student issues. They provide a window on students' daily reality through a safe and familiar framework.

Catalysts may take many forms. They can be relatively formal activities like class rituals, grammar exercises and student research. Alternatively, they can be open-ended activities, with minimal teacher-directed guidance for students' responses. One of the things we've found is that the more instructions, format, and modeling we provide, the more we shape the ways that students respond. While this kind of guidance is sometimes necessary and helpful, it is also important at times for student responses to be completely uninfluenced by teachers' input. Not giving too much guidance is a way of letting go of control; often it results in surprising and interesting responses that lead in directions we never would have predicted. The list below outlines the "ways in" we have explored in our project. It is by no means meant to be exhaustive; you probably already have ideas to add from the exercise you did at the beginning of this chapter. A detailed discussion of each item on the list will follow.

Ways In: Finding Student Themes

1. Setting the tone: Start-up activities to facilitate a participatory atmosphere.
♦ *Our History Book*
♦ Family photos/albums
♦ Family trees
♦ Life journeys
♦ Significant objects
♦ Learning pictures

2. Conscious listening for loaded issues, problems, concerns.
♦ Conversations before, during, and after class
♦ Reading between the lines
♦ What made it hard for you to come to class last week? today?

3. Catalyst activities designed to elicit issues and concerns.
♦ *Grammar exercises: Structured exercises that allow space for students to contribute authentic information from their lives.*
  • "In my country, in the U.S...."
  • Substitution drills: "I'm worried about_____."
  • I need/I want/I like charts
  • Feelings: "I feel angry when_____."
  • Charts (jobs, families, reasons for coming to the U.S., etc.)
  • Superlatives: Easiest/hardest, most/least, etc.
  • Modals: List 5 things that could be better in your life

♦ *Class rituals: Activities that the class does on a routine basis (every day/week).*
  • "Good News/Bad News"; weekend stories
  • Class accomplishments
  • Posted journals
♦ *Student research: Students investigate some aspect of their lives and report back .*
  • Home/community research: Logs on a range of topics
  • Investigating language and literacy use (in the family/community)
♦ *Creating graphics: Students draw, discuss and/or write about pictures reflecting images from their lives.*
  • A map of students' neighborhood
  • Pictures of places students need English
  • "What do you see when you look out your window?"
  • "The house of your childhood"
  • A photo album of students' life in U.S. (to send home)
♦ *Photos, reading, and writing catalysts: Students respond to photos, texts and writing topics through discussion and writing.*

Setting the Tone: Start-up Activities

The key task at the beginning of a cycle is to create an atmosphere of trust in which students feel they can share what's important to them and make the class their own. Activities listed in this section are designed to make students feel that their ideas, experiences, and knowledge are valued. While specific themes or concerns may not emerge from these activities, they are important in terms of establishing a student-centered climate and sending the message that participants' realities provide legitimate content for language and literacy development. Of course, a delicate balance must be struck between inviting students to be open and respecting their privacy: It is important not to put them on the spot with direct personal questions. Drawing students out without being invasive requires sensitivity on the part of the teacher. Some of the ways we've approached this task are:

1. Starting with the impersonal. Madeline began a new class by showing students pictures of newcomers and asking for each, "Why does he want to study English?" Students generated a list of reasons people might want to study; after this modeling with fictional people, she turned the question back to the students themselves, asking "Why do you want to study English?" she got an outpouring of responses.

2. Immediately using student input as the basis for class work. In the same lesson, Madeline wrote down students' own reasons for wanting to study English and used them as the basis for a story which she brought to class the next day. They were thrilled to see that someone had listened to them. It was the first schooling experience these students had had where their own input was valued.

3. Using music. Music creates a relaxed, informal atmosphere and a sense of community, especially if it is music from students' cultures. Learning becomes a game when music is integrated. Raul Añorve uses music in an introductions exercise. Participants form two concentric circles and move in opposite directions while music is playing. When the music stops, they stop and they introduce themselves to the person from the other circle standing opposite them. The same exercise can be done to reinforce grammar points and elicit issues. When the music stops, they complete sentences like, "I'm worried about..." or "I'm thinking about...".

4. Using open-ended grammar exercises that invite student input. Teachers in our project often provided grammar activities that left openings for students to share something from their lives (see pp. 51-52).

5. Sharing something of ourselves as teachers. Loren, who had just had a baby when she started teaching, brought pictures of her daughter, talked about her concerns as a new mother, and wrote about her daughter in class. As a result, students felt more comfortable bringing their own pictures and stories into the classroom, often forgetting teacher-student roles as they shared concerns as parents.

6. Giving students choice and control. If teachers formulate and ask all the questions, the traditional power relations of the classroom are reinforced. Letting students decide what they want to ask gives them some control and allows them to monitor the issue of invasiveness. Ann started one of her classes by asking students to generate a list of questions that they wanted to use to find out about each other. This simple modification of the traditional introductions activity allowed them to determine what they felt comfortable about asking and answering. Andy designed a lesson which allowed students to explicitly formulate their own guidelines for handling personal information in class (see pp. 89-90).

7. Drawing out cultural comparisons. Lessons that elicit information about the students' homelands (e.g., exercises that start "In my country...") are one of the most positive ways to develop students' sense of comfort. Family literacy teachers, for example, often used American holidays as a lead into discussing other holidays, also exploring differences in food, religious beliefs, folktales, and fables.

8. Laughing. There aren't any formulas for this, but making sure there's time for joking and talking about things that aren't important is critical. As teachers, we can set the tone for this by laughing at ourselves, pointing out our own mistakes, and kidding with students. Ann's class, for example, spent one hilarious session just talking about what various animals say in different languages (e.g., "What does a rooster say in Creole?"). One of the biggest mistakes we can make is to try to force the class to focus only on heavy, loaded issues. This is a turn-off for students. They want their classes to be fun, enjoyable, relaxing. Paradoxically, this is precisely what allows us to get to the deeper issues: Making room for what's not important creates the space for people to bring up what is important.

9. Using pictures and graphics. Many of our start-up activities involve responding to or creating graphics that bridge the world of the classroom and the world outside it. Graphics allow everyone to participate regardless of level, contextualizing language through nonlinguistic means.

Our History Book

One of our most successful introductory activities was using a booklet called *Our History Book*, which presents a photo story of the life of an immigrant family. It comes from *English at Work: A Tool Kit for Teachers* (Barndt, Belfiore, & Handscombe, 1991) and works well for a number of reasons: It satisfies students' desire for a "real" text because it is a formal publication with accompanying exercises; the format is clear and accessible, with large photos and a few lines of text per page; its content is authentic and easy for students to relate to with photos of an actual family and the story of changes that immigration brought to their lives; it is a simple but powerful model for students' own stories both because of its form and its content.

Family Photos/Albums

Other forms of linking family photos and writing activities include inviting students to bring or draw pictures of their families or friends, introduce the people in the pictures to the class and describe what they are doing. This is followed by either picture labeling (at lower writing levels) or story writing. It is important here to give students some choices so that students who don't live with their families or don't have pictures of them won't feel left out or upset. Here a student drew a picture of himself because he didn't have a photograph.

Please bring a picture of your family:

Write about your family:

My FAMiLy is THis
I HAVE 1 My MOTHER NOT FATHER is DEAD
I HAVE THEE sistees AND THEE BROTHERS.
My MOTHER Ps MARíA FRANCiBcA CHAVEZ OTERO
My SisTER SHE ARE JOSEFINA, AND CONSUELO, AN FRANCiS
My BROTHERS THEY ARE Jose AGAPiTO, AND FRANCiSCO
AND ViCTOR HUGO THis is ALL My FAMILY

Loren did a variation on this activity: She found 99¢ pocket photo albums at the dime store and collected money to buy one for each student. She asked students to bring in any photos they wanted and put the pictures on the left hand side of the page with some writing on the right hand side. In this case, some students chose to bring magazine pictures rather than family photos. Loren brought her own pictures and did the writing along with students. As a lead-in to the writing, students worked in pairs asking each other questions about the pictures. (Loren said that she found the responses much more interesting when she did NOT model the questions or elicit specific information about the pictures.) When they were done, students put their own pictures with accompanying writing under the cellophane on each page, making a very polished-looking album for each student.

Family Trees

Another useful activity to link students' lives with a vocabulary and language development activity at low levels is drawing family trees. This activity does not require students to bring anything with them and can give teachers a clear sense of literacy levels early in the cycle. Here, the teacher can model by drawing a picture of his or her own family tree (although the danger of modeling is that students may draw their families to look like the teacher's). It may be more useful to provide a range of models—some simple stick figures, some from texts (e.g., Carver and Fotinos, *A Conversation Book: English in Everyday Life, Book Two*, 2nd ed., 1985). The following family tree was produced by one of Madeline's students.

Life Journeys

Students can combine drawing and writing activities in describing their life journeys; this activity entails making a timeline (or some kind of graphic representation) of the important events in one's life and then writing something about it. Again, this form leaves room for choice; some students may emphasize the graphic aspect while others may develop the writing more. A lesson that can be used to start and model your own life journey activity can be found in *ESL for Action: Problem-Posing at Work* (Auerbach & Wallerstein, 1987). It presents the life journey of a refugee named Manh and the story he wrote about it. The following is a description of the way Madeline developed this lesson:

1. Students discussed Manh's life journey, focusing on wh-words.
2. The class generated a list of questions to ask someone about their life.

3. They discussed the context for this type of question—where do people interview you, what kinds of interviews are there, what kinds of questions are OK to ask in which contexts, what kinds of answers are appropriate (safe) in which contexts.

4. Everyone looked at the questions they had generated and wrote down one they really wanted to ask.

5. Madeline modeled an interview. She taped a picture of a Vietnamese man on herself and said,"I'm Manh." She asked students to use their question to interview her. She taped the interview and asked students to listen to the tape.

6. The class voted on how they wanted to conduct their interviews of each other (whole group vs. pairs). They chose to work in pairs, with various groupings (some who could both read and write answers, some who could read only, and some who needed help with the whole process). Madeline worked with the group who needed help with the whole process and set up the tape with the group who could work independently but not write the answers.

7. Students interviewed each other.

8. Madeline transcribed the taped interview, making it into a reading activity for the class. Students commented on some misunderstandings about live/leave/left. Madeline wrote confusing sections of the text on the board; the class discussed reasons for the confusion (the students thought all the questions were about the past because of the prior context of class discussion). This led to a discussion of grammar and why it's important to use tense markers.

As you read the following life journey, think about the themes that emerge for possible exploration.

Significant Objects

Students can be invited to bring in an object that is important in their lives to share with classmates. These objects often prompt students to tell stories that are windows on their lives—who they were in their home countries, what is important to them, who the people in their lives are/were. It is important to give clear instructions and emphasize that the object should be important to the students otherwise students may bring in objects that they have little to say about. The fact that the exercise centers around a concrete object facilitates language use; often the proficiency level is higher than in contrived or textbook exercises because communication about the object is genuine. The section on oral histories in Chapter 4 describes how to structure this activity in detail.

Learning Pictures

When students come to class, they often bring with them conceptions about what education should be based on their own prior learning experiences. For most students, schooling has followed a traditional model with teacher-fronted classrooms, and they have come to see this model as the only valid form of learning. They expect the teacher to be the source of knowledge, to tell them what to do, and to present them with workbooks, fill-in-the-blank exercises, memorization tasks, and dictations. At the same time, however, students in literacy classes have often had negative experiences with this kind of learning: They bring fears and self-doubts. Thus, one of the first jobs of the teacher is to prompt reflection on a range of ways of learning, from formal to less formal, both in-school and out-of-school, and to invite students to examine their own feelings about these ways of learning. This is an important basis for forging a different dynamic in the literacy class.

One way we've done this is through the use of photos—what we call learning pictures. In this activity, the teacher puts out ten or twelve pictures of different learning situations: traditional teacher-fronted classes, people learning in groups with no obvious leader, parents teaching children to ride bikes, children learning from each other, etc. Students are asked to pick a picture that they have a strong reaction to or that reminds them of something in their own lives. They then respond to the picture they have chosen. The form of the response (writing, dictating, talking, working alone or in pairs, etc.) depends on the student's literacy level. After this individual or pair work, students share their stories and compare them. The teacher facilitates discussion, bringing out the notions of formal vs. informal learning. The pictures become the basis for group reflection about how people feel in different settings for learning, how students themselves are teachers and how people learn from each other. The discussion can go in the direction of examining, for example, different ways of learning, student-teacher roles, what counts as real learning or what makes learning a positive experience. It is hard to predict what issues and directions the exercise will evoke; however, our experience has been that it often prompts very powerful and moving personal stories that have the effect of creating bonds among students.

Both the process and the content of this activity set the tone for participatory, nonformal learning because they allow students choice, validate their experience, begin the task of collaboratively constructing knowledge, and make issues of learning and teaching explicit. Loren has written an account of using learning pictures in *Talking Shop* (Nash et al., in press); the issue of dealing with student expectations is addressed further in Chapter 5.

Conscious Listening

In a participatory approach, the teacher is always on the look-out for hot topics that emerge spontaneously when they are least expected. This kind of active listening between the lines is probably the most powerful way of finding students' concerns. This means being tuned into the conversations that occur before and after class, the changes in mood (when students appear distracted, unusually quiet, sad, or nervous), the reasons for absences, and the times when students suddenly switch to their first language. Casual questions, like, "What made it hard for you to come to class last week? yesterday? today?" can elicit information about problems that students are struggling with. Acknowledging these problems and validating the issues that distract students from the work at hand can draw students back into the circle of the class, and increase their engagement and their motivation to participate.

It is important to be sensitive about issues identified in this way; students may not feel comfortable sharing them with the class. At the same time, however, what appears as an individual problem very often touches others in the class in some form as well. In this case, the teacher's task is to find the underlying issue that can be generalized to others and to present it in a form that applies to the whole group without singling out the individual.

An example of finding a theme through this kind of conscious listening occured in Andy's class. One day she noticed a whispered side conversation between two students while the class was discussing how they felt when they spoke English. When she asked the two students if they wanted to share what they were talking about, they recounted a story about being told to speak English in a store. This led to a heated discussion in Spanish about Anglos' fear of immigrants. Andy wrote up the story in English for the next day's lesson. She presents a full account of how the class developed this theme in chapter 2 "Barbara and Ana" of *Talking Shop* (Nash et al., in press).

Themes can be identified from students' writing as well as from their conversation. In one of Loren's classes, students wrote dialogue journals. One day, a student wrote an entry about language use in her family, saying that her husband spoke to her in English but she spoke to him in Spanish because she didn't want him to hear her mistakes in English. Loren recognized this as an issue of relevance to others in the class and asked the student's permission to copy her journal entry (not using her name) and share it with others. It became the starting point for an extensive sequence of activities on language use in the home and community. (The code Loren developed from this is in Chapter 5.)

In another case, Ann noticed that one of her students was upset one day. When she asked him about it, he mentioned that he had made a big mistake at work, ruining a machine because he had used the wrong chemical. He had misunderstood the directions and was worried that his minimal English would get him into more trouble. Ann didn't ask him to share this in class, but instead wrote the following story about the experience of a previous student who had gotten in trouble at work because of a language misunderstanding. By depersonalizing the situation and presenting it to the whole group, Ann created a context where everyone, including the man who was originally upset, could share their stories and strategies. Thus, in this case, a private conversation became the basis for a literacy activity that in turn elicited exploration of a group theme. This discussion allowed the man to see that he was not alone and gave him the opportunity to work on language skills to address his fears.

Please finish this story:

When Carmen came to this country, she worked as a housekeeper in Newton. One Saturday her boss, Mrs. James, cooked a lot of food for a dinner party. She cooked rice and chicken and she made salad. Carmen cleaned every room in the house.

After the party, there was a lot of food leftover. Mrs. James told Carmen to put the food away. Carmen didn't understand. She thought Mrs. James said, "Throw the food away." Carmen threw all the food in the garbage disposal. Mrs. James was furious!

_____

_____

_____

Verbs In the past tense		Vocabulary:	
came	told	housekeeper	put away
worked	said	boss	throw away
cooked	threw	dinner party	garbage disposal
made	thought	leftover furious	cleaned
	was		

Catalyst Activities

Grammar Exercises

Themes can also be elicited in the context of traditional-looking grammar activities. The advantage of these exercises is that they satisfy many students' expectation of what they're supposed to do in class. A fill-in-the-blank or substitution format feels familiar and legitimate to students. Of course, the function of doing grammar work goes beyond eliciting themes; it fits at many different points in the participatory process. A cycle can move from grammar work to an issue or vice-versa. These exercises can be a catalyst for finding themes, a follow-up once themes have been found, or an end in themselves. However grammar work is used and wherever it fits in, the key is to leave room for students to provide content from their own lives. For example:

"In my country/in the U.S..." can provide a frame for work on a variety of grammar points. This kind of cultural comparison leaves the door open for students to present new information while practicing structures determined by the teacher. It is thus a communicative way to practice grammar. For example, students can work on there is/there are with count and non-count nouns by sentence completion exercises (*In my country, there are_____; in the U.S., there are _____.*) They can write or talk about something they were able to do in their country but are not able to do here (*In my country, I could_____; in the U.S., I can't_____.*)

A substitution drill format allows again for student content to be inserted in a controlled structure. In the following exercise, students can substitute their own problems once the pattern has been set.

> **Parent:** I'd like to talk to you when you have time.
> *Teacher:* What's the problem?
> **Parent:** *I'm worried about Tien's homework.*
> *Teacher:* Can we meet after school on Tuesday?

I need, I want, I like, I can, I can't charts can be used to elicit student concerns in the context of working on infinitives, gerunds, and modals. Students can make charts of where and when they need English or of problems in their lives., for example:

I need:	**I want:**
to find a new apartment.	to move to a safer place.
to get a job.	to learn how to drive.
_____	_____

Pictures like those below from *Preventive Mental Health in the ESL Classroom* (Paul, 1986) can be a catalyst for students to practice the language used for stating problems. This may, in turn, elicit students' expression of their own problems and discussion of possible solutions.

There's no heat.　　There's no hot water.　　The stove is broken.　　The lock is broken.

Reprinted by permission of the American Council for Nationalities Service.

Modals: Exercises with *could, should, would,* etc. provide a rich context for eliciting issues. Students can list 5 things that could be better in their lives, they can brainstorm what they would do if they had more money, etc.

The vocabulary of feelings can provide one of the most productive contexts for finding themes, as the following examples show:
♦ Ann did a lesson in which students filled in the blank, *"I feel angry when_____."* Students drew pictures and wrote sentences to go with them. In pairs, they asked each other about their pictures and new issues came out (about difficulties at work).
♦ Loren did a collage activity while working on adjectives; she asked students to cut out pictures of people with different expressions on their faces (showing different emotions). Then students pasted these pictures onto file folders without labeling them. Each student then held up her own collage and led the class by eliciting adjectives.
♦ Andy did a sequence of activities on feelings, combining pictures and sentence formation. She began by showing students photos depicting various emotions and eliciting vocabulary they already knew. This process was interspersed with stories, memories, and associations that the pictures evoked from the students. Andy then presented two sets of cards, one with feeling words and the other with causes or situations that began with "when____." Students then went through a series of steps to match the sets of cards, making "I feel ____ when_____" sentences. Andy included sentences about classroom interactions so that students could discuss "positive and negative feelings about the only experience we all universally shared—our class time together." Finally students made their own sentences. She describes this sequence in detail in *Talking Shop* (Nash et al., in press, p. 5 "Expressing Feelings").

Superlatives are a simple grammar point that provide the context for eliciting issues in a straightforward way. Students can be asked to make sentences using best/worst. (*The best thing about living in the U.S. is _____; the worst thing about living here is _____. The easiest part of my job is _____; the hardest part of my job is _____ . The hardest thing for me to do in English is _____.*)

Charts like this one from *English at Work: A Tool Kit for Teachers* (Barndt, 1986) can be used to elicit content from students' lives and can then become a framework for both grammar activities (e.g., tense work) and finding student concerns.

IMMIGRATION

Name	Where are you from?	How long? (in Canada)	Why did you come?	Do you like Canada? why?
Antoni	Poland	3 years 2 mos.	family problems in Poland	Yes. More food and clothes in Canada.
Lee	Hong Kong	9 years	family	Yes. freedom in Canada. My children like Canada more than me.
Lorenza	Ecuador	6 years	son	Yes. Not too much. I like my country.
Ricky	Hong Kong	5 years	son sponsored me	Yes. easier to save money. when I have money, I can go back
Si Hong	China	3 years	family	Yes. Canada is a free country.

Class Rituals

Another way to integrate an ongoing system for finding themes is by instituting activities that occur on a regular basis each day or week. These can range from a daily ten-minute period when students talk about anything they're thinking about to Monday reports on the activities of the weekend. Calling these "Good News/Bad News" can open the way for students to include not just social activities but also concerns and issues. Teachers can post newsprint on the wall for students to report ideas, events, or questions as a kind of "posted journal" (see Sauvé, 1987). This kind of ritual serves a number of functions besides uncovering themes; for example, newsletters can become reading texts, writing activities, or evaluation tools.

Weekly news: Madeline started each Monday class by writing students' news on newsprint. Sometimes students talked about their weekends; sometimes they focused on news from their home countries. These accounts became the basis of immediate in-class literacy work; Madeline then wrote them up in newspaper format for use in the next class. During one class discussion, students started talking about money and the high cost of living. Madeline transcribed the discussion and brought the text (see below) to the next class. After the students read this newspaper, the discussion turned to wages and why some students' were paid so much less than others. Another issue emerged from this discussion: the extremely loaded and personal issue of green cards. This theme in turn became the content for the following literacy class. Madeline describes the full cycle in "No Green Card, No Good Pay" in *Talking Shop* (Nash et al., in press).

> **GOOD NEWS NEWSPAPER**   **MARCH 22, 1989**
>
> $¢$¢$¢$¢$¢$$¢$¢$¢$¢$¢$¢MONEY$¢$¢$¢$¢$¢$¢$¢$¢$¢$¢$¢$¢
> MARIE-ANNETTE SAID,
> "EVERYTHING IN AMERICA IS EXPENSIVE NOW."
> "IN 1981, HOUSE IS CHEAPER."
> BEFORE, SHE LIVED IN CENTRAL SQUARE ON WESTERN AVE.
> SHE HAD $2^{1/2}$ BEDROOMS AND A BIG KITCHEN.
> SHE PAID $140.
> BOSTON APARTMENTS ARE THE MOST EXPENSIVE IN THE USA.
> MARIE-JEAN SAID,
> "BOSTON IS EXPENSIVE BECAUSE IT GOT WORK."
> MARIE-ANNETTE SAID,
> "HOUSE EXPENSIVE. EVERYTHING EXPENSIVE,
> BUT JOBS DON'T PAY WELL."
> MARIE-JEAN SAID, "JOBS PAY WELL: $7, $8, $9."
> MARIE-ANNETTE SAID,
> "HOUSE GOES UP. EVERYTHING GOES UP.
> JOBS GO UP. BUT NOT ENOUGH."
> $¢
> WHAT DO YOU THINK ABOUT MONEY?
> BEFORE, HOW MUCH RENT DID YOU PAY WHEN YOU CAME TO BOSTON?
> NOW, HOW MUCH RENT DO YOU PAY?
> BEFORE, HOW MUCH MONEY DID YOU GET PAID?
> NOW, HOW MUCH MONEY DO YOU GET PAID?

Class accomplishments: Andy's class developed a "class accomplishments" newsletter which recounted the events of the preceding week for Monday classes. In it, she reported grammar points that were covered, issues that were discussed, and even class attendance. The newsletter served several functions: It was a review and summary for students who had been absent; it helped students become more conscious of attendance issues (even causing attendance to rise). Andy describes it more fully in "Our Class" in *Talking Shop* .

Posted journals: Charo posted a piece of newsprint on the wall which students used to report their daily accomplishments both in and out of class. They wrote on it whenever they felt that they had achieved something that they wanted to report. This became a form of student self-evaluation (see Chapter 8).

Student Research: Adapting Ethnographic Approaches

One of the ways that needs and concerns can be identified with students is by encouraging them to become researchers of their own lives. This means that they ask questions, collect data from their environment, analyze and reflect on the data, and then decide what (if anything) to pursue. Specifically, when this kind of research focuses on language and literacy use in the home, community and workplace, it can become both a needs assessment tool and a vehicle for developing the very practices being investigated, in addition to being a tool for finding themes.

The notion of involving students in research about their own language and literacy use is inspired by the work of Heath and Branscombe (1984). They taught a class of adolescent students who had been labeled "special needs" to become ethnographers in their own communities, investigating language use and literacy practices. Through this process, the students' academic literacy developed to the point where most of them were able to move into college-preparatory classes. Heath claimed that this approach was successful because language and literacy were both the instrument and the object of study: In the process of exploring language and literacy practices (as the object of study), students developed new practices (using them as the instrument of study). Similarly, Lytle, Marmor, and Penner's (1986) work in developing an alternative approach to adult literacy assessment draws from the ethnographic tradition, involving students in in-depth interviews about the actual situations, occasions, types of texts, social contexts, and purposes for reading and writing in their lives.

As we read these studies (which focused primarily on first language literacy), we tried to determine what was and wasn't relevant for our own teaching situations (working with adult second language learners at early stages of literacy development). While the conceptual framework of these studies was enticing, we had doubts about the possibility of putting this approach into practice because of the lack of a common language within classes and the relatively early stages of ESL/literacy of many of the students. However, as we identified the features of the ethnographic approach (outlined in Chapter 2) that contributed to its success, we realized that it corresponded in many ways to our participatory approach. Beyond the general ways that our orientation corresponds to this approach, there were a number of particular types of activities that we adapted:

1. Home/community research activities on a range of topics: By carrying out simple investigations about daily life, students often identify issues of concern. Logs are a simple tool to guide research. Students can keep track of things like: everything that made them happy, sad, angry in one day; every time they need to use English in one day; every place they needed a translator this week, etc. Students who have difficulty writing in English can use drawings to record their observations.

♦ Madeline asked her students to keep a log of all the foods they ate during one week. In the reporting back session, the issue of alar came up: Students had heard reports about apples being unsafe and wanted to know more about the reasons. They did a collaborative language experience story followed by readings and discussions of alar.

2. In-class activities to investigate literacy/language practices/beliefs: Rather than do extensive individual interviews about literacy practices and conceptions (described by Lytle (Lytle, et al., 1986) as an alternative assessment instrument), we integrated activities to elicit similar information in an ongoing way into instructional content.

♦ Andy used a picture of the hands of an old person copying the letters of the alphabet to motivate writing about literacy. The students wrote stories about people they knew who couldn't read and write. A theme that emerged from this was that of literacy networks. Students said you need literacy if you're alone and have to take care of yourself; you need it less if you have families or other people you can depend on.

♦ Ann overheard a conversation about children's negative attitudes toward their first language and developed a code to investigate this issue further (see pp. 70-71). This provided an impetus for exploration of attitudes toward the first language.

3. Linking in-class activities with home/community investigation of language and literacy use: Students discuss some aspect of their own language and literacy practices and beliefs in class and then do further investigation and reflection at home; they then develop their ideas through literacy activities. (Chapter 8 presents a list of possible questions for a language use inventory.)

♦ Students investigated their home contexts for doing homework in several classes. Although each of the classes used a similar catalyst, the issues that emerged were different for every class. In Ann's class, students focused on being tired and having too much housework as factors interfering with helping children with homework. In Loren's class, the focus was more on issues of communication with the school and understanding report cards (see "Homework Codes" in *Talking Shop* (Nash et al., in press). In Madeline's class, students talked about having to hide their literacy problems from their children to maintain their children's respect and having to devise ways of helping their children with school work despite these literacy problems.

♦ Students investigated language choice/use—who uses which language with whom. In the process of exploring this question, themes about family dynamics and roles emerged, as the following entry from a student's journal shows:

> My husband speaks to me in English. And I understand everything he says to me but I don't speak to him in English because I don't want him to see my mistakes because I am embarrassed in front of him. He speaks to me in English and I speak to him in Spanish. Only I speak in English to my daughter and the people in the street or when I go to the hospital or my daughter's school because her teacher speaks English.

Loren asked the student's permission to share this entry with the class (copying it with corrected spelling). As follow-up, students wrote their own accounts of family language dynamics. (A full account of how this cycle developed is presented in Auerbach & McGrail, 1991).

Creating Graphics

Students can be asked to draw or take pictures of significant places, events, or people in their lives. These graphics can become the context for discussion, vocabulary development, and writing activities. In addition, they can become the framework for the elicitation of issues. They can also become the trigger for deepened social analysis, a tool for exploring the issues, a context for extending language and literacy development, and a form of action (these functions are discussed in Chapter 5). Possible subjects for pictures include:

Maps of the neighborhood: After vocabulary and language work around these maps, students can focus on social contextual issues reflected by the maps. Why are there no grocery stores in the neighborhood? How important is the church? What does or doesn't it do? Why are there no banks in the picture? Where are the banks? Do your children go to the neighborhood school? Why/why not? (This technique is used frequently by popular educators in Central and South America to begin analysis of social issues.)

Where do you need English? Where do you use Spanish? Students can draw pictures of all the places they do and don't need to use English. This can become a preliminary group needs assessment that can frame future curriculum units.

What do you see when you look out your window? This exercise can prompt discussion of safety, crime, drugs, play space for children.

The house of your childhood: Students love these pictures and, again, they provide a frame for cultural comparison and the elicitation of issues (e.g., housing conditions). The same approach can be used with other topics (the school of my childhood, etc.).

Photo albums: Students can collect pictures that depict their life in the United States and make them into photo albums to send home to relatives. These pictures provide a window on students' world here.

Photography: Students can be asked to take pictures of significant places, things, or people in their lives as a way of identifying what's important to them. In one site (not part of our Family Literacy Project), students were given a Polaroid camera overnight and invited to take a picture of something important for Haitians living in Boston. These pictures became the catalyst for dialogue and student stories.

Photos, Reading, and Writing Catalysts

Open-ended catalyst activities can include asking students to respond to photographs, reading selections, and writing assignments (or some combination of these) in any way they choose. Students should be able to choose what they want to respond to (e.g., a particular picture or poem) and be asked minimally guiding questions: "What do you see here?";"What does this poem make you think of?";"How do you *feel* about this poem?";"Write something about this poem." Chapter 4 describes in more detail ways of using photos, readings, and writing.

Responding to photos: Photos can be presented singly, in pairs of contrasting pictures or in thematically-based groups. Good sources of photos are books like *The Family of Man, The Family of Woman* (Steichen, 1955; Mason, 1979a, 1979b) as well as calendars from organizations like UNESCO and Oxfam. Loren often gave her students two pictures of families, each with smiling people but from different cultures; her instructions for writing were minimal. Here she discusses her rationale (Nash et al., in press):

> I purposely did not design a set of problem-posing questions to go with the pictures because I wanted to see how the students would read the images without my guidance. I wanted to give them the option of staying in a more labeling or describing mode or to go into a more critical one. I wanted to know if a code could stand by itself without probing questions. What I discovered was that the pictures could indeed stand alone and whether students chose to go deeper and interpret them critically depended on the makeup of the class. It also depended on the level of English, since this was not a bilingual class. (pp. 7-8)

She describes the different ways students chose to respond to them in "Happy Families?" in *Talking Shop* . In one case, the photos served as a rich mine for uncovering issues, while in another they were less productive. About the latter, Loren says, "The use of the pictures provided the backdrop for us to discuss such important issues as: What is happiness? What is wealth? Are these things different in different cultures? Is having money equivalent to being happy? Are people really richer here in the United States? Is it better to be rich or happy?"

Responding to readings: Readings can be used to elicit student reactions and related experiences or as models for students' own writing. Culture-specific forms like proverbs are especially powerful in this regard because they are simple and familiar, yet allow for rich interpetation. In the following example, Ann gave her students a poem to read and then asked them to respond to it with their own poems. Of course, the beauty of the poem is that it's so simple and yet so loaded with meaning, allowing students to take their responses wherever they wished. Ann typed each student's poem on a separate sheet and collated them into a class anthology.

Little Lyric (of Great Importance)
I wish the rent
was heaven sent
                    -Langston Hughes

Here are some poems students wrote after reading Hughes' poem (1974):

I wish tomorrow is a nice day with a blue sky.
And the birds are singing and everybody is happy.
I wish to have a nice car and a house.
I wish to go to college and have good job
In the future
I wish I have my parent and my brother
Here.
I wish I can speak every language.
                    -Bay Sitthirath

I wish I can go back
To my country
Not come
Back anymore
                    -Soutchalith Banthilivong

I wish to eat foods that my
Mother make.
I wish to feel more happy.
                    -Pedro Jucoski

I wish to go to a river with a lot of grass,
Wooded, blue sky, and it has a sidewalk.
To run and to run,
And to listen to the voice of
The water in the river. I think about
All the world and its wonderful things.
                    -Clara Bowley

Writing exercises: Themes can also emerge from student writing, either unexpectedly or as a result of a directed catalyst activity. Dialogue journals are an important place for teachers to get a sense of what is happening in students' lives. (See the section on codes in Chapter 4 for examples of issues identified in this way.) Open-ended quick writing exercises can also lead to the uncovering of themes. In these exercises, students are asked to write freely about whatever comes to mind when they see a prompt. The following catalysts come from a piece of scrap paper I found in my departmental office (with credit to Annie Silverman and Julia Connor, whoever they are!):

♦ a smell you remember
♦ a food that reminds you of something
♦ a place that you love
♦ something you did that you are proud of
♦ something you worry about
♦ something you remember learning
♦ a person who taught you something
♦ a dream that you have
♦ a dream that you had
♦ a time you taught someone something
♦ a time you were afraid/angry/brave
♦ a time you were lost
♦ a time you were punished
♦ a story about yourself five years ago;
♦ a story about yourself in five years

The following example is one student's response to the assignment,"Write about whatever you see when you look out your window." Think about the issues uncovered here as you read it:

...First this is what I told about myself when I finish doing my things around the house. I go to the window and I distract my mind by looking outside. I do that because it is a habit to me. First I don't watch TV. I don't read anything in my house. I don't know why but I don't like to do any of the above. I don't have any time to do that. For me to look out the window is like watching TV. When the police is talking to drug sellers, for me that is very interesting. It is almost every day that this happens. In my mind I think many things when I see these things. I think this is not going to ever stop. The thing that worries me the most is my family, my son, my daughters. This is going to be like that and no one is going to stop it except god. This is like a nightmare.

A Tapestry of Themes

A concern often voiced about participatory ESL is that it may focus too much on problems and thus be negative or depressing for students. Teachers point out that students don't want to think about their problems all the time. However, if teachers genuinely listen to students and center curriculum around content that comes from them, this ceases to be an issue. In fact, once the tone has been set, and students feel that they will be listened to, a rich and unpredictable texture of themes begins to emerge. Dealing with very loaded, global social and political issues is only one aspect of this dynamic. As you read these minutes of one of our staff meetings, note the incredible range of issues that emerged during this one week in the life of our project:

Charo's class: Students in the literacy class at Villa Victoria [a housing development] asked Charo why their Chinese neighbors are celebrating the New Year now. In addition, one of the students has been sick; others have been talking about how sick people manage when they live alone. One woman who lives in V.V. has taken on the role of assisting anyone who is sick—visiting them and cooking for them. Students have decided to use these two issues as topics for their community newsletter. One student will interview Chinese residents about their New Year's celebration; another will interview the woman who watches out for sick people.

Ann's class: One of Ann's students brought in a letter for others to sign about the closing of Brighton High [a high school with a large bilingual program]. She is a Guatemalan woman who doesn't have kids in the high school now but thinks it's important for the whole community to respond. The discussion revolved around why we should do anything even if we're not directly affected. One of the Russian men said he didn't want to talk about it because it didn't concern him; several others argued that it's important because if they cut this program, they'll cut others too (like adult ed classes!); that if high school students lose this school, they'll drop out which will lead to more crime, unemployment and drug use all of which will affect the safety and well-being of everyone else in the community. Others were interested because they had grandchildren at the school; one has a son who is a teacher there. Ann and some students will go to another meeting and get petitions in Vietnamese.

Andy's class: Three of the women in her class do cleaning work so she'll focus on that next week. While she was visiting her sister in Phoenix last week, there was a "sighting" of the Virgin of Guadelupe; community people built a shrine around the tree where she was seen. This was puzzling for Andy and her sister, so she asked her class about it; after discussing it, they wrote a letter explaining the whole phenomenon to her sister.

Madeline's class: Her morning class has been working on the solar system. This came up after a student brought in calendars for everyone following a discussion of the lunar calendar which in turn arose from a discussion on cultural differences in celebrating holidays. The calendars had pictures of the new moon, full moon, etc. After some calendar reading activities, students began to ask about how the solar system works..... (why the moon is full sometimes, etc.). Madeline organized a people model (with students as different planets, etc.) to illustrate the concept of orbits. One woman said she still doesn't believe it and wondered how astronomers know all this—they don't live in the sky and can't see it. This led to a discussion of what you can see in the sky which in turn led to a Vietnamese student telling a folktale that her grandfather used to tell about life after death: After your death you'll be judged if your life has been good or bad. You'll have to walk up the rainbow; it's very hot and if you've been bad, you'll fall off it and be eaten by a tiger or a big fish; If you've been good, you'll be able to walk across the entire rainbow and get to the other side.

Issues

Through the duration of our project we identified scores of issues (grouped into categories below). Although these concerns arose in the context of a family literacy project, they are probably core issues for learners in any adult literacy/ ESL programs.

Culture
♦ *similarities and differences:* holidays, cooking, witchcraft, faith healing, folktales, schooling, religion, weather, employment, family structure, childhood memories

Children's schooling
♦ *safety:* violence in schools and getting to and from school
♦ *discipline (or lack of it):* culturally different approaches to discipline; parents being accused of child abuse, feeling schools aren't strict enough; punishing children for poor school behavior or performance
♦ *fairness/discrimination:* parents' feeling that child is being treated unfairly or neglected
♦ *content/quality of education:* fear that schools aren't teaching enough, lack of communication about what's going on in school
♦ *homework:* ways of helping, feelings of inadequacy
♦ *obstacles to parental involvement:* time (overtime, two jobs); living conditions (homelessness, lack of heat, crowding); other concerns (immigration, family problems, health)
♦ *ways of being involved:* importance of showing concern, advocacy
♦ *bilingual education:* ambivalence (fear of loss of home language and culture; fear of exclusion from mainstream; fear that bilingual education is inferior, segregates children, prevents acquisition of English); lack of involvement in decisions about placement
♦ *social/cultural concerns:* fear about influence of American way (smoking, drugs, sex, skipping school, etc.); fear of loss of culture and control; conflict between home and school values; children's negative feelings about home language and culture
♦ *parent/teacher roles:* teachers asking for more parental support; parents feeling it's the teacher's job
♦ *special needs:* disagreeing with school evaluations and placements; not understanding procedures, rights, implications of placements
♦ *school atmosphere:* feeling unwelcome, not knowing or feeling comfortable with school authorities
♦ *communication:* inability to communicate because of language, lack of translation, inability to understand notes, report cards, etc; only negative communications from school
♦ *afterschool/vacation/holiday care:* problems finding care for children of working parents; finding positive things for children to do while parents are at work; availability, adequacy, cost of daycare and afterschool care

Parents' education and literacy
♦ *educational background:* school stories, conceptions of learning and literacy
♦ *adult literacy:* reasons for coming to school, expectations, uses of language and literacy, the importance and meaning of literacy

♦ *classroom dynamics:* use of first langauge vs. second language in class, attendance, student/teacher roles, personal issues, evaluation of learning
♦ *homework:* contexts for doing it, help from children, obstacles to doing it
♦ *participation in sites:* hiring teachers, evaluation, funding cuts, childcare

Immigration

♦ *experiences and legal issues:* reasons for coming, problems with authorities, hazardous journeys, political and economic situation in homeland, new immigration laws, amnesty and employment implications

Family

♦ *men's/women's roles:* housework, work outside the home; language use; tensions created by changing roles in new culture; women's independence
♦ *parents'/children's roles:* role reversals, loss of respect/authority/control, parents' dependence on children; children as link to new culture, parents' hope; children feeling burdened; mutual support of parents and children; mothering; parents as teachers; separation from children
♦ *language use in the home:* contexts for native language vs. English use; attitudes toward native langauge, emotional significance of language choice; how to maintain native langauge and culture

Neighborhood and community

♦ *quality of life:* safety, loneliness, lack of safe play space for children, mutual support and sense of community (or lack of it); ways of helping neighbors; community issues (school closing, police harrassment); tensions between cultural groups, racism and discrimination

♦ *housing:* finding a place to live, high rents, lack of repairs/heat, overcrowding, condo conversions, tensions with neighbors, understanding cultures of neighbors

Health care

♦ *awareness:* AIDS, nutrition, birth control, lead paint, hazardous workplace chemicals, drugs, drug abuse

Employment

♦ *work:* low pay, having to work two jobs, fear of losing job and not finding new one (immigration law), workers' rights, employers' rights, language problems at work

♦ *welfare:* requirements, impact on motivation and self-esteem, reasons for being on welfare, negative attitudes toward welfare

Politics

♦ *issues:* political situations in home countries, "English Only" legislation, cuts in social services, immigration legislation

5 Tools: Developing Curriculum Around Themes

Once student themes have been identified, the next question becomes how to use them in the classroom. Students may feel that the heated discussions that arise in response to a catalyst are diversions—that they're interesting but don't count as real language work. Our experience has been that the key to legitimizing spontaneous talk or the emergence of issues is the follow-up—consciously keeping track of the "diversions" and developing literacy activities from them. Of course, the kind of follow-up for any given theme will depend on an interaction between the teacher, the topic, and the students. Very often, teachers discover what's appropriate and engaging for students only through a process of experimentation, trying and evaluating as they go. What teachers need, thus, is not a set method or sequence of activities, but what Barndt calls a "tool kit" of techniques, procedures, and activities with which to decide how to develop themes as they are identified. As she (1986) says,

> These tools, are like shovels and picks, to keep you digging away at the rich resources of experience which all adult learners have.They are to help you "mine" the gems of everyday life that become the content of adult learning. (unnumbered pages)

The essence of the concept of "tools" is that students' experience can best be explored through the use of concrete representations of that experience that provide a focus for language work, social analysis, and change. In a participatory classroom, tools are much more than the traditional paper and pencil activities: They are often visual, nonverbal instruments that generate active responses, thinking, and dialogue. Their aim is to engage students and draw them out.

This concept of tools, originating in Freire's work, has been adapted to ESL in various ways. Barndt (1987) uses the term to mean primarily nontextual representations of an issue, because, as she says:

> When we use only verbal motivators to teach language like a text...we keep the focus on what is unknown or uncomfortable to the new speaker of English. A nonverbal tool—like a photograph, a song, or an object—can engage the interest of the student and motivate him or her to talk about a particular theme, taking the focus away from the language issue. (p.13)

Codes—i.e., pictures or texts representing themes—are another kind of tool. Nina Wallerstein adapted this tool for ESL from Freire's codifications in her influential book, *Language and Culture in Conflict* (1983), describing codes as "concrete physical expressions that combine all the elements of [a] theme into one representation" (p. 19). She suggested following the presentation of each code with a structured five-step questioning process. Our own experience is that this format doesn't always work: It may seem too teacher-controlled or narrow in form and direction. The use of other tools opens up this process and provides a greater variety of ways to explore an issue; codes become one possible format among many.

More recently, Wallerstein (1991) has used the term "trigger" to talk about ways of generating reflection, dialogue, and critical thinking:

> ...a trigger is a specific and real example about problematic situations that have personal meaning to people; reflect the individual, community, and societal levels of the problem; and where many solutions are possible... A good trigger is a creation from the listening process that captures the key issues, the emotional meaning of these issues, and the social context of these issues in participants' lives. These

triggers then become the motivational force that lead students to analyze why problems occur, and ultimately to act to prevent similar consequences...through social action. (pp. 10-11)

We use the term "tool" to refer not just to the representation of an issue, but to all the ways of developing themes, combining visual and nonvisual, verbal and nonverbal, textual and nontextual. Tools fall into three categories: those that the teacher chooses from a preexisting source, those that the teacher creates, and those that students are involved in creating. The goal is to move increasingly toward student-created tools. For any given theme, a combination of tools may be used, perhaps starting with a preexisting source, continuing with a teacher-written text, and going on to a collaborative or student-created tool. In addition, tools may become increasingly student-controlled as a class cycle develops through various themes.

The task of choosing and creating tools as new themes emerge is an ongoing one. Thus, when we talk about tools, we are talking about both process and product, about both the model for generating tools and the particular forms they take for a given theme. In this chapter, the focus is more on "how" than on "what"—on the generic processes for creating tools rather than on actual tools resulting from that process. The chart below represents an overview of the tools that will be described in this chapter.

Participatory Tools

for extending language and literacy around student themes presented along a continuum from most teacher-controlled to most student-controlled

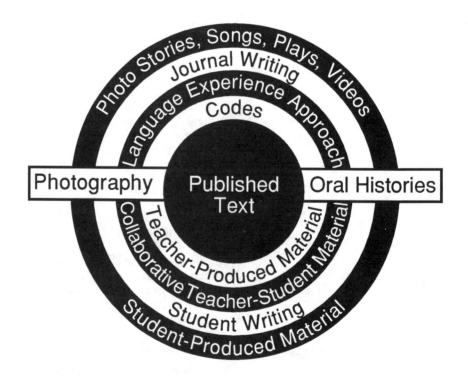

What Are the Functions of Tools?

In looking at this chart, it immediately becomes apparent that the distinction between "ways in" and "tools" is, in many ways, an artificial one. First, the tools that are used in the follow-up phase may look very much like those used to find themes: Texts, photos, or journals may be used in both cases. Second, the line between finding a theme and exploring it further in the classroom is fuzzy; there is not usually a separation between how something emerges and language and literacy work around it. Nonetheless, this distinction is useful because it leaves a conceptual space between identifying an issue and building curriculum around it. While the tools may be similar in form to the ways in, their functions are very different. Where the purpose of the ways in is to uncover meaningful issues, the purpose of the tools is to extend language and literacy proficiency while deepening the analysis of the issues. Barndt, Belfiore, and Hanscombe (1991) call this the difference between "scratching the surface" and "digging deeper."

The dual functions of the tools—both working on language and developing themes on a conceptual level—go hand in hand and cannot be divorced. If either aspect is ignored, the fundamental premise of a participatory approach (that language and literacy instruction should help people to address issues and make changes) is undermined. If a meaningful issue is reduced to mechanical follow-up exercises that focus only on skills, the original motivation for working on language and literacy is lost. Students get the message that content from their lives has little value except as a pretext for language practice. By the same token, if issues are left at the level of discussion, and no explicit attention is paid to language work, students may feel that their linguistic needs are being ignored. Because for many of them talk doesn't count as legitimate language instruction, they may feel that they're not getting their money's worth. Thus, the tools structure the link between the development of language and literacy and analysis/action.

Tools serve the additional function of providing a framework for increasing student participation in curriculum development. As students feel more comfortable, they become involved in the process of producing tools themselves; teacher-created tools become models for student-created tools. Thus, the same form may appear at different points in the curriculum development process, serving different functions and involving different degrees of student participation.

Uses of Photography

The list below shows how photographs can be used as tools serving different functions at various points in the curriculum development process.

Photos as ways in—setting the tone: Students bring photos of their families, home countries, homes, and neighborhoods as a way of introducing themselves and their concerns.

Photos as catalysts: Teachers present pictures without accompanying texts as a way to identify themes and elicit student reactions; students select pictures that they would like to respond to (orally or in writing). Students take photos of significant places, people, or situations in their communities and neighborhoods to identify issues or themes from their lives.

Photos as context for readings: Teachers present pictures with texts as a way to elicit prior knowledge (through prereading exercises), or to provide nonlinguistic information and contextual cues.

Photos as codes: Teachers select a picture or pictures to develop a preidentified issue with guiding questions. Here the picture represents a problematic theme from students' lives and is the frame for dialogue.

Photos as frames for teacher-written stories or LEA stories: Teachers present photos for discussion; students either dictate the story (LEA) or the teacher writes it based on the discussion. The story then becomes a reading text.

Photos as frames for student writing: Students go through the stages of the writing process in response to photos.

Published photo-series: A series of photos that tell a story can be presented:
1. with a predetermined text and follow-up exercises to relate it to students' lives (finish the story, react, rewrite the story);
2. in sequence but without text (students develop the text);
3. out of sequence (in random order); groups can work out their own stories, putting pictures in sequence and developing their own texts.

Individual/class photography: Students or the teacher take pictures of significant places or scenes in their lives (work, home, neighborhood, schools); photos can identify themes or prompt writing and discussion.

Student-produced photo stories: The class creates a photo story as a kind of action. Inside the classroom, students decide on a theme, act it out, take pictures, and write accompanying text; outside the classroom, they identify a community issue, take pictures, and create a text. By developing alternative endings and trying out different solutions, photo stories can be a tool for addressing a problem. The product can become a tool for others in addressing related issues.

As you look at this picture of a kitchen worker in a fancy hotel, think about what issue or issues it represents for students and how you might use it at different points in the curriculum development process.

Reprinted by permission of Tony Loreti, photographer.

Published Texts

A common complaint of teachers is that existing ESL literacy texts are boring. It's hard to find materials that are both simple and interesting enough for low level students. Our experience has been that finding appropriate materials is largely a matter of looking in the right places. There is a wealth of material available from nontraditional sources—authentic texts written for a purpose other than teaching ESL. (We reviewed a number of such texts that we used in our classes in the *TESOL Quarterly* (Auerbach, 1986a). Specific references and ordering information are listed under References and Additional Resources at the end of this book.) We have found that *content* is more important than *level* in determining students' ability to read these materials: If selections are relevant (i.e., students want to read them because they somehow relate to their lives), and are presented in an accessible way, students can read things which, from a linguistic point of view, may seem beyond their level. It is important not to choose only very simplified texts and reject others just because they look too hard. Guidelines for making challenging texts accessible are on the next page.

The most important point to remember in using these materials is that reading is not a pronunciation activity; it is a meaning-making activity. This means that the focus of instruction should not be accuracy in oral reading, but comprehension. If students are corrected whenever they mispronounce a word or read something incorrectly, they will get the message that the purpose of reading is to sound good. Reading research (see Carrell, Devine, & Eskey, 1988) indicates that this kind of sound-centered model of reading inhibits comprehension; proficient readers predict, guess, skip, and often make miscues in the process of reading for meaning. Teachers should ignore miscues unless they interfere with the meaning of the text.

Further, research shows that students' ability to use their prior knowledge is key in comprehension (see relevant chapters in Carrell, Devine, & Eskey, 1988); students can make sense of what they read to the extent that it fits with what they know. Reading must be contextualized in discussion of the text content and structure so that students can establish expectations before reading and read interactively. This can be facilitated by *prereading* discussions and exercises linking text content to student experience, as well as by encouraging students to predict, guess, and skip *during reading*, and again by relating the text to their own lives *after reading*.

Published Materials That Are Nontraditional for Classroom Use

Literature: Excerpts from books, short stories, and poems, especially those by or about immigrants, are powerful ways to elicit student experience. We have used excerpts from Maxine Hong Kingston's *Woman Warrior* (1978), poems by Langston Hughes, and bilingual poetry. See "Images and Stereotypes" in *Talking Shop* (Nash, et al., in press) and Additional Resources, p. 135 of this book.

Oral histories, autobiographies, and biographies: Accounts of real people's lives are engaging, especially when they are ordinary people with experiences similar to those of our students. We have used excerpts from *Don't Be Afraid Gringo: A Honduran Woman Speaks from the Heart* (Alvarado, 1987) (an oral history of a peasant woman who addresses a wide range of issues from domestic violence to education and childrearing) and *The Mango Tree* (Oral History Center, 1987) (a collection of short oral histories by school children interviewing relatives). See "Real People's Stories" in *Talking Shop* and Additional Resources, p. 135 of this book.

Student-produced publications: There is an increasing number of published collections of student writings. Some that we have used are from East End Press (a Toronto-based student publishing house), *Need I Say More* (Boston's journal of adult student writings) and *Voices* (from Canada). See p. 138 for addresses.

Children's literature: In the context of a family literacy class, children's books (perhaps otherwise inappropriate for adults) make sense. They can be read and discusse to model shared reading with children. Multicultural and bilingual books such as those from Children's Book Press in San Francisco are wonderful resources.

Newspapers: Newspaper articles can be used to develop themes or to introduce local issues. We have used articles about a Hispanic parents' organization, the new immigration law, and the English Only movement, making these articles accessible by taking excerpts, dividing the articles into sections that different groups of students read and report on, or re-writing them.

School flyers: Report cards, letters home, parent newspapers, and other materials from students' children's schools can become texts. We have tried to contextualize the reading of these materials in critical literacy activities where students try not only to understand them, but to determine their own responses.

Printed community and workplace materials: Printed handouts, advertisements, signs, bus schedules, employer or union flyers, and other realia that are part of students' everyday environment can become texts. Students can be invited to bring things to class that they need help reading (like the traffic ticket that Madeline's student brought). Again, it is important to address these materials in a critical context, going beyond literal comprehension, with questions like "Why is this written in language that is so difficult to understand, even for Americans?" See "Traffic Tickets" and "Images and Stereotypes" (*Talking Shop*).

Guidelines for Using Published Texts

Choose interesting relevant texts.
♦ Choose passages that clearly relate to students' experiences or concerns (where the topic is familiar, and easily recognizable). Texts written by or about immigrants and those that invite cross-cultural comparison work especially well.
♦ Choose relatively short and pithy excerpts.
♦ Invite students to select from a range of texts or bring in their own.

Use graphic support in presenting texts.
♦ Enlarge excerpts and present them with a lot of blank space on the page.
♦ Pictures, as nonverbal information, can frame prereading discussion.

Before reading: Always present prereading activities.
♦ Elicit prior knowledge: Ask students about their own experience.
♦ Present key concepts and words through clustering exercises: Present a key word and elicit associations with the word ("What does this word/ picture make you think of?"); draw a semantic map or web on the board, linking students' associations to the word in graphic form.
♦ Preview the text and elicit predictions: Look at pictures, the title, and the first sentence and ask students to guess what the passage will be about.
♦ Develop prereading questions with students: Ask students to make their own questions about the passage based on the preview.

During reading: Focus on meaning.
♦ Provide a number of channels of access: Don't stick to the model of one student reading aloud to a group while the teacher corrects. The teacher can read aloud while students read silently; the students can read chorally; they can read silently and then aloud; they can read in pairs.
♦ Break up the reading of a passage: Present short pieces of it at a time (making predictions and discussing meaning as you go) or have groups of students read different sections and share them with others.

After reading: Link texts to students' experience.
♦ Ask for students' interpretations rather than only literal comprehension.
♦ Ask students to evaluate what they read in light of their own experience ("Does this seem real? Has anything like this ever happened to you? What would you do if...?"). They can tell or write their own sentences, poems, or stories related to what they read.
♦ Have students do read/react exercises: On the left side of the page, they copy a passage they liked, disliked, had strong feelings about, or that reminded them of something; on the right side, they write their reactions.
♦ Ask students to generate questions for the story's author or each other.

Fables, Folktales, and Proverbs

Fable, folktale, and proverb genres are particularly effective in meeting the goal of using published materials to draw out students' own experience. Although the specific content varies from culture to culture, the forms are familiar to most cultural groups and many of the themes are universal. As a result, they provide a powerful framework for cultural exchange.

Fable and folktale activities are particularly suited to family literacy classes as a way into parent-child interactions; sharing these stories can serve as a model for the kind of sharing that parents might do with their children. Stories written by parents can become a vehicle for preserving and transmitting the home culture. For example, in one class, Ann's students read a bilingual Punjabi/English fable; then she gave them a blank lined page with the heading, "A Fable from_____." Students responded in a variety of ways. One wrote a fable from her country and read it in class with her child. Another copied something from a children's book. Another wrote a song from her country. One wrote about the history of her own country, and still another wrote about a personal experience in her country. In another class, Ann presented a fable about wishes and a worksheet; students wrote their own wish stories modeled on it.

There are currently several ESL texts with fables and folktales from different countries (e.g., Kasser & Silverman, 1986); these can be adapted in a number of ways:

1. Before reading, talk about what a fable is (i.e., a story with a moral or lesson, often using animals to represent people). Model and elicit oral examples.
2. Do a literacy activity, e.g., present scrambled sentences of the story on cards (like a strip story); ask groups of students to put them together
3. Present the text as a whole, in the way it appears in a book or in simplified and enlarged form. Students can read it silently or chorally, or listen to the teacher read it.
4. Students can work in small groups with questions about the story, or they can generate their own questions for each other.
5. Follow-up can take a number of forms:

   ♦ Students can tell and then write stories from their own cultures that the text reminds them of.
   ♦ Groups of students from the same culture can work together to produce a story collaboratively and then share it with the class.
   ♦ Students can share language games, songs, or stories they tell young children, in their home cultures.
   ♦ Students can make books to share at home based on these stories.
   ♦ Students can respond in whatever way they choose.

Teacher-Produced Materials

Teachers can create class-specific materials based on themes they have identified by listening to students. The teacher writes a short text that raises an issue without presenting a solution. Texts can take the form of short stories, dialogues, "Dear Abby" letters, or news articles, followed by discussion questions, grammar work, or writing exercises. As the following examples, created by Ann, show, they can be used as a way to generate discussion of alternative solutions, situate a local problem in a broader context, or elicit new issues.

September 21, 1987

Dear Frances,

How are you doing? I'm writing now to ask your advice. You know I was working in the Comfort Pillow Factory in Somerville. I had some problems one day while I was working. The boss said I was talking too much when I was at work. It isn't true, but anyway he fired me last week. Now I need to find another job.

Yesterday when I was walking downtown I saw a "HELP WANTED" sign in a restaurant. I thought it looked good, But last night I was talking to some friends and my friend Alicia said that I can't get another job because of the new immigration law. My friend Allen said I should go to the Immigration office and get amnesty. I am scared and confused. Do you have any suggestions? Is it easy to find work in New York City? Please write soon!

Your friend in Boston,

Jean-Paul

Example: This teacher-written article was accompanied by vocabulary work and the following questions.

ANN LANDERS

Dear Ann Landers:

I'm in a bind. I hope you can help me out. I'm a mother with two kids in the Boston Public Schools. My oldest child is 15 years old. She is taking a Health class. In the Health class they are teaching the kids about AIDS. I am very angry. I think my daughter is too young to learn about this. Another problem is that I don't speak much English so I can't talk to the teachers. Please help!! What should I do?

signed

a very angry mother

What?
- ♦ AIDS is Acquired Immune Deficiency Syndrome.
- ♦ It is a sickness without a cure.

Who?
- ♦ Anyone can get AIDS—old, young, male, female, heterosexual, homosexual.

How?
- ♦ A person can get AIDS through sexual contact and from contaminated intravenous needles.
- ♦ AIDS is spread when blood or semen are shared.
- ♦ A person *cannot* get AIDS through casual contact (kissing, shaking hands, toilet seats).
- ♦ Pregnant mothers can give their babies AIDS.

What can we do to prevent AIDS?

- ♦ We can educate ourselves and our family and friends.
- ♦ We can use condoms and birth control gel with Nonoxynol 9 when we have sexual contact.

You make friends with someone from another country who recently moved to Boston. Your new friend does not speak much English. He asks you about AIDS. "What is AIDS? How can people get AIDS? How can I avoid getting AIDS?" Can you answer his questions?

Do you know anyone who has AIDS? How do you think you would feel if someone you know got AIDS? What would you do?

Some people say "People who get AIDS are bad." Why do you think they say this? Do you agree? Why or why not?

Codes

The most important difference between a code and other teacher-created materials is that a code presents an issue in very concrete, simplified form, accompanied by a structured series of dialogue questions leading to social analysis and action. A code may be verbal (a short dialogue or text) or non-verbal (a drawing or photo). The mark of a good code is that it generates heated discussion. A code is much more than a visual aid: it is a framework for critical thinking. Here are the guidelines for codes and dialogue questions adapted from Wallerstein (1983):

Guidelines for Codes and Dialogue Questions

A code should be:
- **familiar:** represent a clearly recognizable daily concern
- **emotionally charged, loaded:** represent an issue that evokes emotion, invites involvement and response
- **two-sided/problematized:** represent a problem or contradiction, presented in a way that is complex enough to show its various contradictory aspects but simple enough for students to project their own experience onto it.
- **open-ended:** without any implied solutions or obvious right/wrong interpretations

Dialogue questions should follow this five-step sequence:
1. **Describe** what's happening: What do you see? Who do you see? What are they doing? This is the literal comprehension phase.
2. **Define** the problem concretely: What's the problem here? Students name the problem and talk about its various aspects. There may be several views of the problem which get redefined through dialogue.
3. **Relate** it to individual experiences: Has anything like this ever happened to you? Do you ever feel like X? What happens in your country/ neighborhood/workplace? Sometimes it helps to ask indirect questions like, Do you know anyone in a similar situation? This gives students the option of masking their own experience.
4. **Analyze** root causes: Where did this problem come from? Why does it exist? Who created this situation? As students look for causes, they situate the issue in a broader social/historical context.
5. **Plan for action:** What can we do about the problem? Students develop their own alternatives for addressing the problem, figure out ways to take action and discuss consequences of different strategies.

Examples of Codes

The following is an example of a teacher-made code with questions simple enough to use with beginning students (from Paul, 1986, p. 31). It shows that you don't have to be an artist to draw codes. Barndt even suggests that teachers draw codes with their left hand if they're right-handed (or vice versa) to demonstrate that it's not the artistic quality of the picture that counts, but the clarity of the content. This may make students less inhibited about drawing their own codes as well. Another excellent source of codes with simple questions is *In Print* (Long & Podnecky, 1988).

This activity was developed in response to the large number of harrassment incidents in many refugee neighborhoods. The ESL students are told that the woman looking out the window in the picture below has a hospital appointment she doesn't want to miss, in a little over an hour's time. Use the following progression of questions to guide a classroom discussion:

I. Describe content:
- What do you see?
- Who is the woman?
- What is she doing?
- What is she thinking?
- Where is she?
- Who are the men?
- What are they doing?
- What are they thinking?
- Where are they?

II. Define problem:
- How does the woman feel?
- Is she happy, sad, worried, afraid? Why?
- Why is she alone?
- How do the men feel? Why?
- Do they like to stand in the street?
- What does the woman think the men feel?
- What do the men think the woman feels?

III. Personalize problem:
- Has this ever happened to you?
- How did you feel?
- Did you leave the house?
- Did you talk to the men?
- Did they talk to you?

IV. Discuss problem within a socio-economic/cultural context:
- In your country/culture, are people alone much?
- Are they afraid?
- Do women walk in the streets alone?

Reprinted by permission of the American Council for Nationalities Service.

The following code, dealing with the issue of children's negative feelings about the home language, resulted from an overheard conversation between a parent and child. It can be used with non-Spanish-speaking students by asking them to guess what Lucia is saying.

Lucia: Vámonos, pues.
Maria: I don't want to go with you.
Lucia: ¿Porqué no?
Maria: Because you always talk in Spanish. It sounds stupid. When you speak Spanish, everyone knows we come from Puerto Rico. Why don't you talk to me in English?
Lucia: Tu familia habla español. Debes sentirte orgullosa de tus raices.
Maria: English is better. All my friends speak English. Anyway, I don't understand Spanish.

DIALOGUE QUESTIONS

1. Who do you think Lucia is? Who do you think Maria is?
   What language is Lucia speaking?
   What language is Maria speaking?

2. What language does Maria want her mother to speak? Why?
   What does Maria think about Spanish?
   Does Maria want people to know that her family is from Puerto Rico?
   Does Maria understand Spanish? Why does she say she doesn't?

3. How would you feel if Maria were your daughter?
   Do you know anyone who feels like Maria?
   Do you know anyone who feels like Lucia?

4. Why do children resist their parents' language?
   How do schools view your language?
   Where do children get their attitudes toward languages?

5. What can parents, children, or schools do about this problem?
   What can we do in our families?

Using Codes

Codes can be presented in a number of ways: asking students to take parts and act them out, scrambling lines or cutting them apart and asking students to put them together; as cloze exercises, etc. Breaking them down and presenting them as language lessons may make them more accessible and satisfy students' desire to focus on language work.

The questions and guidelines for discussion should be seen as just that—guidelines—and not as prescriptions. Their purpose is not to give students language practice but rather to provide teachers with a conceptual framework to guide discussion so that critical thinking develops. This means the questions don't have to be presented to students in writing. Without conscious guidance, it is very easy for the discussion to get stuck at the level of relating codes to students' personal experience. What differentiates a problem-posing approach from others is that it goes beyond personal stories to examine individual experience in light of collective experience and even further toward making changes in light of the analysis. Thus, teachers should use the questions to keep on this general track, but also should feel free to rephrase them or change the content, maintaining the general direction from description to experience to social analysis and strategies for change.

As with any tool, what actually happens when you present a code may be quite different from what you planned. A code may fail to spark any interest or it may raise completely new issues. Further, the stages of the dialogue process may not all happen at once or in discussion format. It may take weeks to go through the process of moving from the introduction of an issue to the action stage with a range of activities along the way. It is important to include concrete language work at various stages (especially in focusing on action), asking not just "What can you do?" but also, "What can you say?"

Finally, it is important to involve students increasingly in creating their own tools: photos, texts, skits, etc. Teachers' codes, thus, serve as a model for what students themselves may produce. Guidelines for developing codes with students are presented in *ESL for Action* (Auerbach & Wallerstein, 1987).

Collaborative Teacher-Student Materials

One of the most powerful tools for following up on the discussion generated by catalysts, published texts, or codes is creating texts from students' own words and ideas. Seeing their own words written, photocopied, and presented as reading material gives students a real sense of the importance of their ideas. It also legitimizes talk that students might otherwise feel doesn't count as real language learning. For many students, it is the first time that they have had the experience of seeing their own words in writing. Because the words and ideas are theirs, the text is already familiar, facilitating the link between sound, symbol, and meaning. Madeline's lowest level classes could read much longer and more complicated texts than when they were based on class discussions. Further, the conceptual level of this kind of text is often much more sophisticated than anything students encounter in published literacy materials for beginners.

In addition, as students see what they have said in writing, they make connections between spoken and written language. As teachers model the process, collaborative writing becomes a step toward independent student writing. Classroom roles change as the teacher shifts from being the generator of meaning to being a scribe. Finally, when students' own words are re-presented to them, they can reflect on what they have said, leading to further analysis.

Guidelines for the Language Experience Approach (LEA)

Getting started: Elicit ideas and establish a purpose. Because LEA is designed to reinforce the connection between print and meaning, content is key: Students have to have something to say! If it's clear that students already have a lot to say—they're engaged in a heated discussion—the teacher can ask if they want to write their ideas, giving them a choice and establishing a purpose for the activity (with questions like "Would you like to write a group letter about this?"). Or, the teacher can initiate the LEA process with brainstorming or clustering exercises: Students call out as quickly as possible any words that come to mind about a phrase, picture, or key word. Once a few of these words have been generated, each in turn becomes a catalyst for new words or phrases; as students generate clusters of words, the teacher writes them up in a web of relationships from which a story emerges. Since the point of this stage in the process is to generate ideas, it is extremely important to be flexible about language choice. The content of the story and what students attempt to say in English will be more complex and meaningful if they have the option of developing ideas in their first language.

Writing the story: Focus on content, not form. The main concern in writing should be expressing ideas. Elicit content with questions like, "What's important in this story? How do you want it to start? What do you want me to write? What comes next?" Try to avoid putting words into students' mouths. If students see exactly what they say in writing, they will make connections between oral and written language. If they are corrected, the flow of ideas will be inhibited, the conceptual level of the content will be diminished, and the link between speaking and writing will be undermined.

Reading the story: Move from supported to independent reading. The teacher can read the text aloud as she writes it, read sentences and paragraphs when they're done, and invite students to read along. When the story is completed, the teacher can read it back to students as they read silently, asking them if they want to change anything and pointing to each word as it is read. The class can read the story chorally; then students can read sentences or the story individually or in pairs.

Follow up activities: Extend language and ideas. What you do with a story once it's written depends on its purpose. The teacher can ask, "Which words do you like/not like?" to identify themes and provide vocabulary for further individual student writing. If the story is to be shared with an outside audience, students often want to revise and edit it. They can cut sentences into strips, group and reorganize them. If the story is for internal use only, revising may be counter-productive. The biggest danger in follow-up work is reducing a meaningful task to mechanical skills work. If key words are taken out of the story for phonics or vocabulary work, they should be put back into meaningful sentences in which new ideas are generated. Questions should go beyond checking comprehension to extending thinking around the theme so that the story generates more reflection, dialogue, or action.

Collaborative writing can be used in a variety of contexts, with different degrees of student participation. The teacher can take notes non-intrusively during a spontaneous discussion or write them from memory after the class is over; the notes then serve as a text for further reading and discussion. In this case, the ideas come from the students but the actual words are chosen by the teacher. Alternatively, nonintrusive transcribing can be done in front of students, so that they see key words and ideas as they emerge. Again, the generation of ideas is not disrupted by involving students in the actual writing (focus on form) but the literacy link is immediate, with the record of the discussion available for follow-up later. Finally, the teacher can explicitly invite students to dictate a story or discussion, using a Language Experience Approach. In any case, the key to using this tool is linking it organically to the development of a theme rather than seeing it as an isolated activity or an end in itself.

**A Clustering Exercise and an LEA Story
Generated in Response to a Picture**

everything   good   important in life
                                  important in
                                    the world

          education — school

reading and writing   feel ashamed
                             but it's not your
                                        fault
  I don't have
                             parents'
not enough schools   fault
not enough teachers
not enough freedom   parents can't
                             afford it

          some don't care

This is a picture of a school. The picture has a blackboard. It has a teacher. It has students. students looking at the blackboard. She's writing math. The teacher looking at the blackboard. "No good, writing." He is angry. No nice teacher. Student is afraid for teacher. School no good. Teacher is not happy because students don't understand. Teacher says, "write more, write again."

An LEA Cycle

While Madeline was working on a food and nutrition theme in class, she did a clustering exercise about the word "apple". Someone mentioned that there was a story on the news about apples being unhealthy and was concerned about this because their children ate a lot of apples. Madeline rewrote a newspaper article about alar. This, in turn, generated a discussion about causes of the problem and strategies for addressing it. Madeline took notes on the discussion and used it as a further text. In this example, the sequence moved from an LEA activity to a teacher-written text to a collaborative text. The article and collaborative text are presented here.

Many Apples Still Tainted with Alar

Many apples grown in the U.S. might be tainted with Alar.
Maybe 33% of all apples grown in the U.S. might be tainted with Alar.
Alar might cause cancer.

A TV show called 60 Minutes tested 200 apples from supermarkets from all over the U.S.
The reporter from 60 Minutes found Alar in many apples.
The reporter found Alar in:

    38% of red apples
    32% of all apples
    30% of apples called Alar-free.

Many farmers said that they don't use Alar anymore, but the reporter found that many farmers still use Alar.

Alar helps apples to stay fresh for a long time.
Alar also helps apples look nice.
Alar might increase your chance of getting cancer.

People should just stop buying apples. If they don't eat apples, they won't die. The farmers will stop using Alar.

People do things that hurt themselves. They don't care if they eat things that are dangerous. They take drugs, etc.

Maybe the newspapers are making the story big. I never heard about someone dying from eating apples.

The government should stop the Alar.

Student Writing   For adult literacy students, writing is often the most neglected skill area. They are given few opportunities for anything but the most rudimentary, functional kinds of writing: filling in blanks, forms, and writing sentences for the purpose of grammar practice. The focus of these tasks is arriving at the correct form of some predetermined content. The rationale is that these are the only kinds of writing tasks students really need and are capable of until their language develops. Writing, like reading, is often construed as a bottom-up process where each subskill (e.g., letter formation, spelling,) must be mastered before proceeding to the next level.

Our experience has been that often students enjoy the challenge of writing from the earliest stages of literacy development and are able to express meaning very powerfully even with limited vocabulary and literacy proficiency. When the focus is on content rather than form, mechanical difficulties with letter formation, spelling, and grammar seem less like insurmountable obstacles. Of central importance is talking about writing as a meaning-making process with students to overcome their deeply instilled concern with correctness. Here, a beginning level student expresses a powerful contradiction in her life.

> my name is Batheemise
> My country is Haiti.
> Before I was Business
> Now I am restaurant worker.
> *woman.*

Thus, even in beginning classes, it is important to provide opportunities for students to write for real purposes and audiences. They may start with picture labelling or sentences based on content that comes from their lives. They may do personal writing (journals), interpersonal writing (letters), intergroup writing (exchanges of texts), or public writing (stories, poems, articles, letters for publication). In any case, the emphasis is on communicating ideas and creating semantically whole texts. In addition to stressing writing for real purposes, a participatory approach emphasizes writing as a social rather than an individual process; students draw on each others' resources in generating and developing ideas, expressing them in a new language, working on organization and mechanics, and sharing the products of their labor. They work together to figure out what they want to say and how to say it, help each other when they're stuck, use each other as audiences and readers, and celebrate producing a final product. These ideas come from the writing process approach, which has become popular for elementary, secondary, and college levels, but which is less often applied to adult ESL. They go beyond the writing process approach to the extent that they incorporate critical social analysis and action for change.

Guidelines for Process Writing with Students

Getting started
♦ Contextualize writing, linking it to discussion and content students are already engaged with; writing should be one mode for expressing ideas, not an end in itself.
♦ Choose topics with students, not for them: Don't predetermine topics; as a theme emerges, ask students if they want to write about it. The more control students have over what they write, the more they will become involved in the writing.
♦ Use concrete forms to generate ideas: Students can respond to visual or verbal catalysts (photos or reading excerpts) or create their own drawings or skits. Rachel Martin (1989) suggests asking students to call out titles to a picture (which the teacher writes on the board); then students write the story behind the title. She also suggests that students compare their own stories to the original when pictures have a text with them.
♦ Provide a model of the format: A visual model (a piece of writing in similar format or a page set up with lines) helps students structure their writing.

Developing ideas
♦ Use key words/phrases to develop ideas and vocabulary: Write emotionally loaded ideas on the board as discussion of a theme develops.
♦ Use visuals: Charts, clustering exercises, and maps can help students schematize ideas.
♦ Freewriting/free talking: Have students write or talk in pairs about anything that comes to mind on a theme for a few minutes; then elicit ideas from the group.
♦ Use interviewing: Have students generate questions, interview each other to elicit ideas.
♦ Allow language choice: Since the goal is to use writing to express meaning, students should be given the option of using the first language to develop ideas.

Drafting
♦ Use class time for writing: Students become models for each other as they see each other write. They can ask each other for help and talk about their work as they write.
♦ Write with students: If you write while students are writing, they see that you are going through the same process; sharing your messy drafts and difficulties dispels notions that good writing involves writing perfectly the first time around.

Responding and revising
♦ Decide whether to revise: It's not always necessary to develop a piece of writing to a final product. In some cases, just getting an idea out may be enough. Decide whether to refine a piece on the basis of its purpose: If students want to develop an idea or share their work publicly they will probably want to revise it.
♦ Make revising a social process: Ask students to read their drafts to each other; just the process of reading her own work may give the writer ideas.
♦ Focus on content and ideas: Rachel Martin suggests asking questions like "What's the most important thing you're saying? What just came into your head as you're reading? What do you want to do next?"—questions that leave control with the writer.

Editing
♦ Leave editing until the end: Don't work on mechanics until students have expressed their ideas the way they want them; otherwise the flow of ideas may be inhibited.
♦ Edit selectively: Decide on a few key points so students aren't overwhelmed.
♦ Encourage self-editing: Ask students to find problem areas to develop monitoring skills.

Publishing
♦ Type, copy, collate, or distribute student writings on a theme when possible.
♦ Use student publications as texts for further reading, to share with other classes.

Guidelines for Journal Writing

Student journals are an informal way to engage students in personal writing and to establish one-to-one communication with them. They give students a place to express ideas without worrying about form and teachers a window on students' lives that can lead to the identification of issues.

♦ Provide bound notebooks with lined pages for students to write in. We used bluebooks because they are cheap, small enough not to be overwhelming, but official-looking.

♦ Explain to students that journals are for writing anything they want to write about and will be a place for the exchange of ideas, not for grammar work—that you are concerned with their thoughts, not with spelling, punctuation, etc.

♦ Journals should be self-selected writing only, not a place for other kinds of writing assignments. To get the ball rolling, though, you can suggest that students write a few words or sentences about themselves, their lives, or something that has happened recently.

♦ Include time for journal writing in class on a regular basis (e.g., 15 minutes at the beginning or end of each class or once a week). Make the atmosphere relaxed: Loren played music during journal time.

♦ Hand journals back to students as quickly as possible.

♦ Respond to students' writing by sharing your own thoughts, experiences, and feelings. This kind of sharing (rather than commenting only on students' experiences) creates a sense of equality and exchange. Experiment with asking students questions; sometimes it may be too controlling and sometimes it may help students continue writing.

♦ Negotiate the issue of corrections. Students often want teachers to correct their journals. It's important both to explain why you're not correcting and to accommodate their desire for corrections. Some possible ways of doing this are modeling a correct form by giving back a sentence with the same structure but different content; asking students to underline the words or forms they want corrected and giving them the correction on a separate piece of paper (not correcting the students' writing itself); selecting recurring problems or problems that interfere with meaning by designing lessons to teach those structures.

Autobiographical Writing

Focused writing about specific themes in students' lives elicits rich stories. Our students wrote about their mothers, their journeys to the United States, their own school experiences, their own teaching and learning as parents, language use in the family, and family dynamics. Most of these writings were in response to another task—reading someone else's story, drawing time lines, reacting to a picture, reading a poem or an excerpt from literature. "Writing About Our Mothers" and "Real People's Stories" in *Talking Shop* both describe teachers' experiences doing this kind of autobiographical writing with students. The following example is from a unit called "Mothers Are Teachers," in which students took pictures of their children and wrote about ways they teach them. It was later published in *Need I Say More* (Publishing for Literacy Project, 1988).

ABOUT NATALY RUBIO

By Gloria Rubio

I wanted to say something about my wonderful little girl. Her name is Nataly, she is 2 and a half years old. She is a very nice girl, she is very sweet, she smiles alot.

Two weeks ago I started to teach her how to use the toilet. The first day when I started to teach Nataly about toilet training, I told her, "Nataly, it is time to leave your Pampers because you aren't supposed to use Pampers anymore. You are a big girl now." So I explained to her, when babies are bigger they don't need to use Pampers anymore. She hasn't used Pampers since that first day.

She is a very nice girl. She tells me every 10 or 15 minutes, "Mamy, I want to make peepee," and she goes to the bathroom and uses it very well. That same day in the night I tried to put the Pampers on Nataly for the night, but she didn't want them. She told me, "Mamy, I don't want to use Pampers. I don't like Pampers." Before she went to sleep she went to the bathroom and she told me, "OK Mamy, I'm all ready to go to bed," and she slept without Pampers. She didn't have anymore accidents in the bed. Sometimes when I stay outside of my house with her, she tells me that she needs to go to the bathroom.

From the first day of training to today Nataly is doing everthing well and she likes using the toilet. I'm happy with her. (p. 41)

Reprinted by permission of the Adult Literacy Resource Institute.

Letter Exchanges

The process: Inspired by Heath and Branscombe (1985) and others, we decided to set up letter-writing exchanges between classes. Each teacher introduced the idea to her students in a group discussion, explaining it as a way to get to know other immigrants and refugees in similar situations. When given the choice about participating, some were enthusiastic and others reluctant because they felt they couldn't write well enough. Teachers pursued the idea with those classes that seemed most interested. Participating classes did class profile charts including information on each student's name, age, sex, home country, and neighborhood in Boston. We decided not to elicit other kinds of information (about work, children, etc.) so that these topics could become part of the content of the exchange. Making these charts itself was a language development activity (e.g., clarifying the difference between address and neighborhood). Classes were then paired on the basis of size (corresponding numbers of students) and they exchanged class profiles; students in one class used the available information to choose partners. Students then talked about, wrote, and sent off their first letters (through their teacher, who delivered them to the partners' teacher).

Some problems: As soon as this initial process was completed, a number of logistical problems began to emerge. Answers didn't come back soon enough and senders got discouraged by the lack of immediate feedback. The class pairings were uneven: Higher level students were disappointed with their partners' letters; the matching within classes was somewhat random so students didn't always have common interests. The content of many of the letters seemed formulaic; students hadn't internalized the idea that the kind of letter you write shapes the response you get. The purposes for writing were not clear, either to us or to the students, in terms of what students would get out of it and how it related to other things we were doing; some students seemed to be doing it because it was an assignment. Other things (e.g., day to day problems) took priority for the class and for individuals: It was hard to fit letter-writing in.

Finally, class cycles weren't long enough to fully explore the possibilities of this kind of exchange; by the time partners had been chosen and one round of letters had been exchanged, the cycle was over and a new set of students were in class. Without the support of the classroom context, it was difficult for students who had moved to higher levels to sustain the writing.

A different kind of exchange: Following up on this effort, Loren started an exchange between her class (Hispanic mothers) and that of a friend who was teaching pregnant and parenting Hispanic teens in another part of the state. The purpose of the exchange was framed as giving advice and sharing concerns about parenting. Loren noted that the resulting letters were the longest pieces of writing her students had done—significantly more elaborate, detailed, and authentic than others. In this case, there was a commonality of experience and a clear purpose for the exchange.

In another case, her class did an exchange of stories about parenting with an ABE class (mainly African-American mothers). Each group wrote about the issues they were facing as parents, and read each others' stories. One student from Loren's class visited the other class and read her work aloud. Writings from the two classes were pulled together into a booklet about parenting, which in turn became the focus of a workshop at a city-wide conference for literacy students. The workshop was an exciting one: In addition to the two classes meeting, a group of Indochinese women from another site came. Everyone was astounded by the fact that despite differences in background, culture, and language, the issues they faced were so similar: their fears for their children about drugs, AIDS, schooling and so on. Clearly, in these two cases, it was the content of the issues that pulled the groups together and gave the exchange its power.

> *Some implications:* These contrasting experiences suggest the following:
> ♦ It's not enough to set up a letter exchange for its own sake; there needs to be some content-related motivating reason.
> ♦ In the initial pairing process, both level and interest need to be taken into account. Group interest and commonality of experience are as important as individual interest.
> ♦ Class time must be devoted to exploring possible issues and topics, developing a sense of audience (with students pairing up to explore what's interesting to another person) and modeling letter-writing.
> ♦ Issues that draw students away from personal letter exchanges can be incorporated into letters once suitable partnerships have been established; students can write about issues that are consuming their energy.

Class and Community Newsletters

Class newsletters serve several functions. They can summarize classroom activities, discussions, and learning for students who have been absent; they can provide review; they can legitimize past discussions and catalyze new ones; they can be a vehicle for communicating with other classes in the same site; they can be a form of documentation of learning; they can be a tool for developing a participatory atmosphere. Teachers can begin by writing articles themselves, then write collaboratively with students until eventually students take over the process, including the production itself.

Charo's class, located in a housing development, produced a community newsletter that contained articles on community events, interviews with community members, and reports on what was happening in class for non-students who were interested. One issue, for example, included an interview with a community person who visits tenants when they are sick, articles about Chinese New Year (because many tenants are Chinese and the Hispanic tenants were curious about their celebrations), an article about a tenant who visits people in prison who have no family in this country, stories about several other residents, and news of those who are sick (so others could look out for them).

Public Writing: Letters, Speeches, Testimonials

Public writing can take many forms: letters to the editor or to public officials, speeches, or testimony for public hearings. This kind of writing, written to real audiences for real purposes, is among the most authentic and powerful types of writing for adult students. Our students wrote letters to teachers, newspaper editors, funders, and government officials on many occasions. The following letter was written to the Governor of Massachusetts at the time of funding cuts.

Student-Produced Projects

Perhaps the most participatory tools are those that students produce themselves, from beginning to end, combining various media and genre. In these, students decide not only on the theme or content, but actually carry out the production process right up to the final product. Projects may take the form of photo stories, photo novellas (a Latin American genre which might best be described as a soap opera in comic book form using photos instead of drawings), soap operas, sociodramas, songs, videotapes, and slide shows. Ideally, students take responsibility for both creative and technical aspects of the production process. In a photo story, for example, they decide the storyline, take the pictures, write, revise, and edit the text, select and sequence the photos, design and lay out the final product. This process is empowering because it puts control of the technology as well as of the content in the hands of the learners; through it they learn technical and organizational skills.

The processes involved in this kind of project are complex, variable, and time consuming; for each form (photo novellas, photo stories, video productions, participatory theater, etc.), there is a substantial literature documenting the rationale, procedures, and accounts of implementation. Since the best models for doing this type of work are the examples themselves, it makes more sense to refer readers to them (see Additional Resources, p. 135), rather than present guidelines here. A good starting point is Barndt's *Just Getting There*, which provides an overview of the range of possibilities, including examples of using photo novellas to reflect on classroom roles; using sociodramas to enact and reflect on relationships and situations of women's daily lives (e.g., being homebound, raising adolescents, etc.); using songwriting and cartoons to address a workplace problem (e.g., machines breaking down); using photo stories and drawings to frame analysis of roles in immigrant families; and using photo stories to explore the issue of finding work. With our own students, the closest we came to this type of process was a photography project, the FOCUS project, undertaken by one of Loren's classes and written up in a separate volume (Strohmeyer & McGrail, 1988). The following excerpts from *On FOCUS* give a sense of the power of this type of participatory project. (Unfortunately, *On FOCUS* is currently out of print.)

FOCUS: A Photography and Writing Project

The first time we met as a group, we spent a good amount of time discussing the project and its possible outcomes. All the participants expressed why they were there and what they expected. This type of discussion took place many times throughout the duration of the project. We then plunged right into an exploration of images and how we react to them, utilizing some Polaroid slides of familiar scenes to the students: objects, people, and corners in and around El Centro where the program is located. This activity served the dual purpose of introducing students to the different elements of photography, i.e., light, focus, composition, etc. and providing them with the sense that, as photographers, they are empowered to choose how they want to present their subject. What followed is what set the stage for the rest of the project. There is something to photography in terms of its abstractness that allows people to conjure up an opinion, especially when there are no words attached to the image. Regardless of their level or language ability, not a single student in the class proceeded to just describe factual information of what was in the picture, but instead, wrote what the image evoked in them...

Several exciting things happened in the second cycle. Angel, a student who had participated in the project the previous cycle, joined us. He was instrumental in guiding the other project participants through several activities. For instance, he trained the new participants on the use of the Polaroids, and also, on different occasions, he talked to the students about his experiences the previous cycle, setting the stage for photo and writing activities. Something else that happened this cycle is that students were interested in developing photos and writings around a theme. Out of this cycle, emerged the "units" on *Mothers are Teachers* and *Neighborhood*, marking a difference from the "free form" works of the first cycle...

Letting go and releasing our imagination and creativity was the most fun. For some of us, FOCUS was refuge from bureaucratic hurdles..., from personal problems, from stolen welfare checks, from custody battles, from our war-ridden countries, and from our set daily routines and habits. Instead, we allowed ourselves to look at all these realities from another perspective by stepping back and looking through a different lens (p. 6).

Reprinted by permission of Loren McGrail and Beatriz Strohmeyer.

Oral Histories

We end this chapter with oral histories because, like photos, they can be used in many ways for many purposes at different points in the curriculum development process, and can thus serve as a kind of recapitulation of the range of possible tools. We were fortunate to participate in several workshops by Cindy Cohen and Beth Ensin of the Cambridge Oral History Center; most of what is written here is based on these workshops. (The Oral History Center's address is listed under Additional Resources, p. 135.)

Narrowly defined, oral history is a research methodology that involves listening to and documenting stories told by ordinary people about objects, people, places, and events in their lives. Historians collect these stories as the basis for historical analysis; anthropologists see them as a window on culture; folklorists collect them as unwritten literature. What's different about their use in ESL classes is that the process of collecting stories becomes a tool that benefits the storytellers themselves.

Why Use Oral Histories in the ESL Classrooms?

Our students are the bearers of incredible stories. Inviting them to share these stories with each other can be powerful for many reasons. Immigrants come to ESL in the process of leaving old ways behind; they may feel ambivalent about where they've come from, especially in a new culture which all too often sends the message that in order to "become American," they need to forget their pasts and "be like us." The process of sharing stories becomes a validation of the past, a way of reconciling the old and the new; by telling their stories in English class, students' own cultures become a bridge to the new language.

In terms of classroom dynamics, the process of telling these stories itself builds trust among students. It helps students communicate across barriers of race, culture, and gender and takes the focus off the teacher as students work together. In terms of language learning, sharing stories creates an atmosphere of genuine communication where language is used for a very real exchange of information and feelings. Since it doesn't require a final, written product, it can be used to develop listening and speaking (as well as reading and writing) and can draw on different learning styles (visual and oral) and be used at different language levels. Most importantly, it involves students in communicating about and creating something that matters to them, that has meaning in their lives.

As Beth Ensin of the Oral History Center said, the greatest gift you can give someone is to listen to their story. Listening is the central component of the oral history process. But listening is by no means a passive activity as we usually think of it: the way you listen in an interview can either silence the storyteller or draw out a story. The kind of active listening required for oral history interviews is a skill that must be learned through practice and reflection. What follows is a description not just of how to listen in an interview but of learning how to listen based on our own workshops with the Oral History Center.

The Process: Doing Oral History Interviews

Selecting a topic: An interview must have a focus (more than "tell me your story"); very often it helps to center the interview around something concrete (an object, picture, timeline, map, or smell). Our own interviews focused on objects and important people in our lives. Topics can also come from classroom interaction: In Loren's class, the question "Have you ever had the experience of God listening to you?" came up in discussion; she thought this would have made a wonderful topic for interviews.

Other topics might include a favorite food, ways of cultivating, weather, childhood mischief, animals, smells (bring bags with distinct-smelling things like coffee and ask what memories or stories they evoke), a time when you went through a change, a journey, gifts, school experience, stories your mother told you or stories you want your children to remember from your homeland.

Brainstorming possible interview questions: Once a topic or theme is selected, participants can generate possible questions to guide the interview. It is important to stress that these are guiding questions, not a rigid format that must be followed. For the interview about "an important person in your life," questions we generated included:

♦ Think of an older person in your life.
♦ Can you remember a story they used to tell you? Something they always used to say or some advice they gave you?
♦ Where do you know them from?
♦ How would you describe them?
♦ Has your relationship with this person gone through any changes?
♦ What is special about this person? Do they have any special talent or skill?
♦ What do you mean to this person?

For the interview about an object, participants are asked to bring in or draw an object that is important to them; we generated the following questions for this topic:

♦ What is this object?
♦ How did it come into your life?
♦ Where is it usually kept?
♦ Who else uses it besides you?
♦ Why is it important to you?
♦ What will happen to it in the future?
♦ What are your memories of things you've done with this object?
♦ As you look at it, what does it make you think of?

Modeling, observing and reflecting on an interview: Once questions are generated, the workshop leader can interview a volunteer while participants observe the interview, noting what the interviewer does in the listening process. After we did this in our workshops, we noted the following ways (both non-verbal and verbal) that the interviewer let the interviewee know she was listening:

♦ Maintaining eye contact
♦ Not interrupting
♦ Allowing for pauses and silences (without needing to fill them)
♦ Smiling, laughing
♦ Using body language; sometimes lightly touching the object or person
♦ Repeating or restating to affirm what the story-teller said
♦ Asking questions that directly followed-up on what the storyteller said
♦ Acknowledging the emotional content of what the storyteller said ("It sounds like you have a lot to say about that." "That must have been very painful for you.")
♦ Not sticking narrowly to the predetermined interview questions but letting curiosity guide the questions; the interviewer can ask about anything that interests her.

Issues: In addition to these observations, we discussed issues implicit in the process that interviewers need to be sensitive about, including the following:

♦ Certain kinds of nonverbal behavior may be culture-specific such as touching or eye contact.
♦ Certain kinds of questions may be culture-specific or seem invasive to the storyteller; it is important always to leave an out, telling people to feel free to decline to answer a question; be sure to teach "I'd rather not talk about that."
♦ There is a danger of imposing one's own interpretation on what the storyteller is saying by restating or reformulating it; in addition, restating can be perceived as saying it better or as appearing to correct.

Interviewing each other: After observing and discussing the model interview, participants can sit in groups of three, taking turns being the interviewer, the interviewee, and the observer; they are asked to remember points where they felt nervous, uncomfortable, or unsure of what to do. This process of doing our own interviews and reflecting on how it feels to be interviewed deepened our understanding of the reasons for some of the listening behaviors and issues in doing interviews.

For example, a common feeling among interviewers was a fear of crying or of silence—not knowing what to do when people get emotional, start to cry, or are suddenly silent. Beth stressed giving interviewees the choice to talk or not to talk when a loaded issue first shows itself (with questions like "Do you want to tell me about this?"). Our impulse is to fill the silence, but a lot happens during the silence: Emotions come to the surface. Another impulse may be to try to fix a problem or say something to make the person feel better, but Beth said that it is often enough to experience the emotion with the person. It is important to remember that talking about a traumatic experience is part of dealing with it and, in this case, just listening to someone is a gift in itself.

Oral History Activities

The process presented above may serve as a model that teachers can adapt for ESL students. (In *Talking Shop* "Oral Histories," Ann Cason describes what happened when she did this with one of her classes.)

There are other ways to involve students in oral history work, from reading histories produced by others, to becoming the subjects of interviews, to doing their own interviews, to creating oral history products. While many of these activities are similar in form, their purposes are different. Classes may focus on only one of these or move through them sequentially.

Setting the tone/Finding themes: Oral histories can be used to create an atmosphere of trust in the classroom; in this case, the purpose is to encourage students to share something of themselves and to listen to each other (rather than to produce a finished product). The teacher may use this time to focus on listening for important issues and concerns in students' lives (to be developed through other activities).

Reading existing oral histories: There are a number of wonderful published collections of oral history stories that can be used as reading material to introduce the idea of oral histories or as models for texts that students might write themselves.

Story-telling: Before doing more formal oral history interviews, students can be involved in telling or writing their own stories.

Teacher-conducted interviews: The teacher can model the interview process with one student in front of the class. The students can generate a list of questions to ask, observe the model interview, and discuss the interviewing process. The model interview can also be taped and transcribed for further language work; the tape can be used to teach transcribing skills with more advanced classes.

Student interviews: After observing and discussing interviewing, students can choose a theme, make up questions together, and interview each other in class. This activity can be an end in itself or the basis for other activities (presenting each other's stories, taping, transcribing, etc.).

Guest interviews: The teacher or students can invite a community person to class and interview him or her either as a whole class or in small groups. Again, a taping and transcribing component or a less structured follow-up writing can be added (e.g., a story or newspaper article).

Community interviews: Students can go out into the community to interview community people. They can start by making a class list of people whom they would really like to find out about (e.g,. people who know how to do something that they would like to do or who have a special skill; people who have been in this country longer than they have; people who have dealt with issues they face—schooling, housing, parent advocacy, etc.). They can share tapes and include transcribing activities.

The Product: Presenting the Oral Histories

The culmination of the oral history activities may be creating a final product; these products can take many forms, incorporate a range of skills, and reflect students' culture, becoming a rich tapestry of cultural diversity. In any case, the more that students take over the production process, the more participatory the curriculum becomes.

Exhibits: Photos and objects and the stories that go with them can be displayed in the literacy center, a local library, or school.

Photo stories: A class can publish a collection of oral histories (with or without photos) for use by other students, in children's schools, etc.

Portfolios: Photos and stories of people in a class or center can be collected in binder form as a growing resource for ongoing use (generating a site-specific set of histories).

Children's books: Individual stories from the homeland can be printed and bound (with hand-sewn binding) as volumes to bring home, to give to children's schools or to libraries, to leave at literacy centers for childcare, etc.

Quilts: Students can each quilt a square that tells a story; squares can then be sewn together into a large quilt, which is displayed with accompanying stories.

Paper quilts: Students can do drawings or other artwork of experiences with accompanying stories (same as above only on paper).

Murals: Students can paint murals depicting scenes from their own histories, homelands, experiences coming to the United States, etc. These painting projects can be accompanied by oral histories that students collect themselves or that have been collected and transcribed by others.

Storytelling celebrations: Other classes or community people can be invited to an event at which objects/photos/artwork are displayed and stories told or read.

Radio shows: Stories can be taped in radio show format with music.

Slide shows: Students can take slides of people telling stories with objects/photos/community sites, and an audiotape of the storytelling to accompany it, with music, etc.

Video tapes: Same as above, with videos of storytelling.

Add your own:

6 Issues From Practice

In this chapter we're going to take a brief intermission between the tools and the action stages in curriculum development to look at some recurring issues that arise in the process of finding themes and exploring them through dialogue and literacy activities. As soon as we started our own work with students, we began to confront questions like: How could we find student issues if their English was minimal? How could the classes be participatory if students expected a traditional, teacher-centered classroom? What should we do if an issue seemed too hot to handle? Or if students used their first language in class? This chapter will examine some of the issues that will no doubt confront anyone involved in putting a participatory approach into practice. More importantly, it will suggest a process for addressing them as they come up.

Your Practice...

Before proceeding, discuss and list some of your own questions, reservations, and doubts about the approach described so far in this book. If you have begun to implement some of the ideas, discuss the problems or teaching issues that have arisen for you.

♦ When were you at a loss to know what to do next?
♦ When did you feel a conflict between your expectations and those of your students?
♦ When was there a problem in classroom dynamics?
♦ When did you feel uncomfortable?
♦ When did you feel constrained by external factors over which you had no control?
♦ How did you handle these questions and concerns when they arose?

Our Practice...

Conflicting Agendas

What if students want a traditional, teacher-centered class? Very often the only model of education that adult literacy students are familiar with is the very model which has excluded them in the past: the teacher-fronted transmission-of-knowledge-and-skills model. They think that learning is only legitimate when it involves worksheets, grammar exercises, linear progression through a textbook, drills, and tests. Teachers are supposed to talk and students are supposed to listen or respond. They may see discussions as diversions from "real" language work and view attempts to involve them in decision-making about the curriculum as a sign of the teacher's incompetence; if we ask for student input about activities or directions, the response may be "You're the teacher; you should know—whatever you think is best."

This poses a dilemma: If we claim to follow a model centered around student concerns, what do we do if their initial concern is to have a teacher-centered model? If we're genuinely participatory, shouldn't we do what they want? Aren't we imposing our own view if we don't follow their wishes? In responding to this dilemma, we must first remember that students make this choice often because it's the only model they've been exposed to; they don't know there are alternatives. Secondly, we have to keep in mind that the model students know is also likely to be one that they have had little success with—it may be the very reason that they have literacy problems! In order to address this dilemma we need both to respect student wishes (so as not to impose a model they're uncomfortable with, which would reinforce a "teacher-knows-best" dynamic) and to give students experience with concrete alternatives as a basis for making informed choices. Some ways of doing this are: mixing the old with the new; explicitly focusing on conceptions of education as curriculum content; having students act as teachers; and including classroom dynamics as content. (For a discussion of including students in ongoing evaluation, see Chapter 8, Evaluation: What Counts as Progress?)

Mixing the Old With the New

Students and teachers both need to feel safe in the classroom and often traditional roles are the most comfortable for everyone. It is important to acknowledge this need and not feel that we constantly have to be innovative, breaking the rules in every lesson. The key is not to scrap all the tried and true ways, but to push ourselves to take risks, asking "How is what I'm doing different from what I've done before?" For us, this has meant mixing traditional forms of instruction (grammar exercises, fill-in-the-blanks, etc.) with less familiar forms. Very often it's not so much the materials being used, but how they're used that differentiates a participatory curriculum from a more traditional one. Lessons can be set up so that the teacher provides a structure, but content comes from the students. Madeline adapted lessons from *Side by Side* and *Line by Line* (Molinsky & Bliss, 1983, 1988) by simplifying the grammar, enlarging the print, and asking students to relate the content to their own experiences. Ann did the following lesson combining work on the phrase "used to" with drawing out (literally) information on holidays.

Ann started by talking about Thanksgiving, what the holiday is and what she used to do with her family. Students corrected a story about Thanksgiving using "used to." Ann asked students to tell about holidays in their countries. Students talked about what they "used to" do for those holidays. They drew pictures and wrote sentences with "used to" about the holidays.

Paradoxically, as the following example from our teachers' meeting minutes shows, sometimes students' refusal to do something that the teacher sees as student-centered may show that the class is becoming genuinely participatory and student-centered—that students feel real control in the classroom.

> In one of Madeline's classes, students resisted the idea of writing personal stories about education in their homelands because they said they wanted to work on grammar: they were able to do this precisely because they knew that they could determine the direction of the class. In fact, when Madeline began a lesson similar to Ann's with a story about her Thanksgiving vacation as a way to work on the past tense, they spent the entire two hours talking about holidays in different countries. She wrote up this discussion which became the basis for more grammar work. What struck her was that although students said they didn't want to focus on their own stories, they couldn't stop telling them and, in fact, saw them as perfectly legitimate when they were framed as grammar work.

Reading, Writing, and Talking About Different Approaches to Education as an Explicit Part of Curriculum Content

An important aspect of moving from one model to another is sharing educational experiences and expectations. As students reflect on their past education, both formal and informal, they develop an awareness of what worked and didn't work for them. Here are some ways we did this:

Student-taught lessons: Students can be invited to teach the group something that they are good at; in one of my classes students taught lessons on corn-row braiding, cooking a dish from their country, relaxation exercises, word games, and phrases from their language. This role reversal serves several purposes: It provides an authentic context for communication in English (language work!); it causes students to think about what they know and are good at; it provides a forum for cultural sharing; it prompts a reconceptualization of who has knowledge in the classroom and promotes the exchange of this knowledge; it invites students to think about what helps people to learn; and it's fun—it creates a relaxed and interactive classroom atmosphere. Teachers can follow this kind of lesson with questions like: What makes it easy for you to learn? What did you learn most quickly and why? In one of my classes, students came to the realization that learning is easiest for them when it is connected to something that they already know.

Learning pictures: Using photos as catalysts for sharing experiences, students can reflect on the many ways of learning, expand their view of what counts as education, and set the tone for continuing to talk about approaches to language and literacy acquisition. See Chapter 4 and *Talking Shop,* (Nash, et al., in press) "Learning Pictures" for fuller descriptions.

School stories: Students can also write about their own experiences after reading other people's published stories about schooling. The following story was written by one of Ann's students:

> When I was 5 years old, I like to watch the children going to school. I remember one day I asked my mother, "Why don't I go to school?" and she answered me that I was still a child.
>
> My house was near the school. So one day, I went to school by myself. When I met a teacher, I asked her the same question, "Why can't I come to school." and she answered, "Because we don't have enough desks." "After that, I went back to my house, and the following day, I took a small, old chair from my house, and I went to school. When I entered the classroom (it was the fourth grade) all the children watched me and started to laugh at me. I started to cry and cry immediately.
>
> The teacher asked me, "What are you doing here?" But I couldn't say anything because I was crying so much and I decided to go back home and forget about school.

Making classroom dynamics into instructional content: Another way to bridge the gap between a traditional and a participatory approach is to develop lessons around issues of classroom dynamics. In this way, students can express their ideas about how classes should be run (even disagreeing with the participatory mode if they wish) and make changes in this community. Bringing classroom issues back to students for discussion, reflection, and decision-making reinforces their sense of control and takes the teacher out of the position of authority.

In the following excerpt of teacher meeting minutes, Andy talks about a time when she made the issue of using personal information into a topic for classwork. This dialogue enabled students to reflect on what they had been doing, give some feedback, and take some action (in this case, the decision not to do something was a form of action).

> Last month, a student suggested that we start a suggestion box, where students could present their ideas anonymously. For a while, no one made use of it. Then, one day, we found the following message, written in Spanish except for the parenthetical phrase: *Certain teachers ask about our lives in class (I don't like it). There are ways of teaching English that don't require finding out about someone's life.*
>
> I brought the issue into the classrooms for group discussion, where most people assured me that personal discussions were interesting for them and that they felt that the assignments left room for them to be personal or impersonal as they liked. They told me that the degree to which they reveal personal information was their choice. "Nobody have to say what they don't want."
>
> However, there were a couple of assignments that made them uncomfortable—specifically, those that involved recounting the history of how and why they came to the United States. They were particularly disturbed by an assignment that a non-teaching staff member gave them. In an attempt to promote our center and the cause of Hispanics in Boston, he pushed them to write their personal stories for a public newsletter.

Their anger and confusion over this request did not surface until the personal information suggestion was under discussion. Their grievance was brought to the staffperson's attention. He came to the class and rephrased his request so that the students better understood his motivation and their option to participate or not. To date, none have written anything for the newsletter.

Our teachers often made issues of classroom dynamics into codes. For example, Andy presented the following code after she noticed a tension between students who attended regularly and those who missed classes and then required review.

Nidia: This class is boring. I wish the teacher would do something new.
Juan: I like it. I wasn't here last time so this is new for me.
Nidia: Well, why don't you come to class regularly so that we don't have to review all the time?
Juan: Sometimes I miss the bus from work and the next one doesn't come for an hour.

She reported that the result was better communication between the two groups, increased empathy, and no more tension; in addition, there was more peer tutoring and less class time spent on review.

When some students wrote, "The teacher should make some people be quiet and others talk" in a class evaluation, Ann drew a cartoon of a classroom with four frames; the same person is talking in each frame and increasingly more students are falling asleep. The cartoon prompted a discussion about uneven class participation (see *Talking Shop,* "Group Dynamics" for a full account of this lesson).

Working with Low-Level Students

How can we find and explore student issues if students can't express themselves in English? One of our big concerns early on was that that there wouldn't be much we could do in a participatory way with low level students because of their language limitations. Madeline, in particular, had students from various language backgrounds with minimal English and L1 literacy skills. Although she reminded us about the reality of these constraints when we talked about finding and exploring themes, she also constantly pushed herself to develop ways of adapting the model with these students. The following principles guided most of our work with low level students:

Break things down or simplify them in terms of form but not in terms of content. The point here is to make print accessible without diluting its meaning or making content childlike. In the parking ticket example, Madeline simplified the mechanical aspects of the composing process while pushing conceptual development to a higher level. Other ways teachers in our project did this include:

1. On a graphic level:
♦ Starting with non-language-based materials (using open-ended pictures to which students can bring their own words and interpretations; having students draw and label their own pictures);
♦ Using the photocopier to enlarge text excerpts;
♦ Rewriting passages by hand in large print;
♦ Leaving a great deal of blank space on the text pages;
♦ Providing a format for exercises.

2. On a linguistic level:
♦ Rewriting highly meaningful, loaded passages in simplified language (for example, rewriting a newspaper headline).

3. On a decoding level:
♦ Using content that's meaningful and drawn from student experience, like key words related to the homeland.

4. On a textual level:

♦ Doing prereading and prewriting activities through which students develop a conceptual and schematic framework for building meaning;

♦ Breaking longer texts into sections and assigning them to different students.

Never underestimate your students. Our experience has been that when students are interested in the content of a lesson, they are capable of doing much more than we may expect. Time and again, when we were worried about material being too hard, we found that students responded well if they were interested in it. Levels are inherent neither in materials nor in students: Students' ability to handle material depends as much on their interest in it and how it's presented as on language factors as the following minutes show.

> Ann reported that she tried using the "Family Story"—a cartoon version of a student story about the division of work inside the home. She was apprehensive about using this material because of the language level and because the format is quite complicated. The students responded enthusiastically, taking on the roles of different people in the story, acting out and discussing a variety of endings for the story. Ann felt that it turned out to be positive that the material wasn't easy: it gave the students something to struggle with and because the content was meaningful, they were able to overcome the format and language difficulties.

The following exercise was done around the time of the 1990 Haitian elections. Madeline asked students to think of any word that came to mind when they heard the word election. She wrote the words (many of which were cognates in (French, Haitian Creole, and English) on the board; from these, students identified four key words. She used these for another clustering exercise from which the class generated the following chart. In this exericse, students generated a sophisticated political analysis at a highly developed conceptual level despite a relatively low level of English language proficiency.

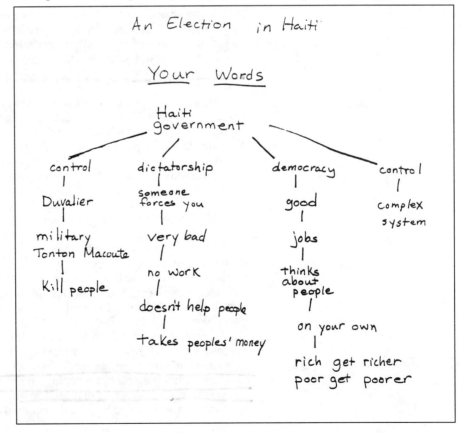

Teaching Grammar

Doesn't grammar get neglected in a participatory approach? The issue of whether and how to teach grammar is a complicated one. Many people are concerned that students won't learn grammar if the focus is on issues. In fact, students themselves may see a grammar-driven curriculum as the only legitimate approach to language learning. At the same time, however, traditional grammar lessons may confuse students, particularly those who have little education or literacy in the first language. They may not have the metalinguistic or cognitive awareness—the experience of talking and thinking about language as an object, with categories and rules—that facilitate grammar-based learning. No matter how much students practice grammar points and get them right on controlled exercises, they may continue making the same errors in less controlled contexts.

Of course, there is a vast literature in second language acquisition research about this question claiming that learners go through successive stages in grammatical development (called interlanguages) and only acquire what they're ready for at a particular point in this development. Some argue that unconscious acquisition is a more powerful process than conscious learning. Others argue that adults, in particular, are able to benefit from conscious learning because of their cognitive development. To complicate matters further, both learners and teachers bring to class their own varying expectations, learning/teaching styles, and prior experience. In any given classroom, some students may want explicit grammar instruction while others may be completely lost or bored by it.

Where does all this leave the teacher? One of my graduate students once said that her mother used to give the dog aspirin rolled in peanut butter and that this is how to teach grammar—disguise it! Others say the opposite: You have to make grammar instruction explicit so that students feel that they are getting what they want. Our experience lies somewhere in between. It is certainly a misconception to say that grammar should not be taught in participatory ESL classrooms. Although there are no simple how-to's for teaching grammar, the follow guidelines may help teachers struggling with this question:

1. Remember that issues, not grammar points, should be the driving force of the curriculum. This means that in a participatory approach, although there may be a general sense of an appropriate grammar sequence, (e.g., starting with the simple present and past tenses before conditionals), decisions about lesson content should be determined in terms of content, not narrowly in terms of grammar.

2. Identify grammar to be taught through observation of language use. As students write and talk about issues, the teacher can note recurring grammar problems to use as the basis for follow-up exercises. Teachers do not need to respond immediately to errors (since this may interfere with communication) but may save the response for later. Or, if communication breaks down because of a grammar problem, the teacher can help to clarify it, later using this information to devise an exercise built on the theme, providing practice with the structure.

3. Always contextualize grammar. Once grammar problems have been noted and selected for instruction, they should be re-presented in a contextualized way, connected to the issue from which they emerged. For example, past tense exercises can be developed from weekend stories or cultural sharing about women's work in the home country vs. in the United States. Writing process educators have developed mini-lessons as an instructional tool; the mini-lesson is a short (five-minute) focused intervention in which the teacher explains a particular point and invites students to focus on that point in subsequent work. Again, timing is key: If the intervention interrupts the flow of dialogue, it sends the message that form is more important than content. However, if grammatical problems and errors are never addressed, students may feel they aren't learning. Remember that the point of focusing on grammar is to improve communication about issues: it is not an end in itself. It is important, therefore, not to stop with the grammar work but to go back to the original issue that motivated it.

4. Use a range of formats, leaving grammar exercises open-ended. Provide structure but leave space for student-generated content in developing exercises. This means that after structures have been modeled, students can be invited to contribute information from their own lives to complete exercises. (see p. 51-52 in Chapter 3 for examples.) The formats can include games (e.g., Twenty Questions, Jeopardy, team games), scrambled stories, cloze exercises, and others that are familiar in more traditional ESL classes.

5. Diversify the points where grammar is introduced. Once grammar instruction is conceived of as more than decontextualized verb tense exercises, but as an active, targeted language focus designed to enhance communication, the range of times and ways to introduce it can be expanded. Content-rich grammar exercises can be introduced as a way in to finding themes (e.g., simple present tense exercises like *I get angry when____*); as a follow-up to dialogue about a code (e.g., a cloze exercise based on the transcription of a class story); as rehearsal for action (e.g., a competency format for complaining about a problem at work); or as a frame for evaluation (e.g., *always, sometimes, never* sentences about the class and program). (See the example below.)

6. Discuss the issue of grammar instruction with students. Finally, at the risk of sounding like a broken record, I want to reiterate the value of bringing up the issue of grammar instruction with students. Like other issues of classroom dynamics, this one can be negotiated with the teacher and students sharing perspectives. In this way, the responsibility for determining how much and when to teach grammar doesn't rest only on the teacher.

The example, on the next page, originally developed by Lenore Balliro and adapted by Ann, could be used early in the process to elicit students' own problems, in the middle to link a code to particular situations, or toward the end to develop the language for action.

Adapted from an exercise by Lenore Balliro.

Using the First Language

What should the teacher do if students use the first language (L1) in the classroom? The traditional assumption is that the first language should be used as little as possible in an ESL class. This assumption rests on the notion that students will learn the second language better if they are forced to express themselves in it at all times (although research evidence on this issue is not conclusive). Very often teachers feel it is their responsibility to make students stick to English; they become the enforcers of an English-only rule in class. This, however, creates two problems in a participatory approach: First, it reinforces the role of the teacher as authority figure; second, it makes it more difficult to find themes and promote conceptual development with low-level students. This issue can also become a source of tension among students. Some may feel more comfortable learning English through the first language and may use the first language frequently in class. Others may feel that it's being used too much—they're in class to learn English.

Our experience is that letting go of the notion that using the first language is always bad relieves much of the tension around this issue for both teachers and students. More importantly, the first language can act as a powerful bridge to the second language and can promote literacy and conceptual development. While people usually ask a yes-or-no question about this issue —"Should the first language be used in an ESL class?"—we concluded that the questions should instead be "What are the functions of using the first language? How and when should the first language be used?" Some of the functions of using the first language in our own classes were the following:

- to find themes;
- to explain learning strategies or grammar points;
- to talk about language and literacy, to develop metalinguistic awareness;
- to give directions and get clarification;
- to develop meaning, concepts, and critical thinking about an issue;
  (This emphasizes that it matters that what a learner says in English is meaningful and that a learner can develop his or her ideas in L1 before expressing them in L2.)
- to talk about very loaded emotional topics;
- to promote the bonding of the group;
- to translate words so that communication isn't interrupted.

However, it is not enough for us to determine when it is and isn't helpful to use the first language. If we come up with a new set of "rules" for language choice, we are continuing in our roles of problem-solvers or enforcers. Rather, the key is figuring out with students in what ways the L1 helps or hinders class goals, when they want to use it and when they don't. Because language choice is a problem of classroom dynamics, it makes sense to deal with it in a problem-posing way. Exploring this issue with students enables them to develop conceptually and set their own guidelines, taking the teacher out of the role of authority. When the decision is in their hands, students become monitors for each other.

Loren used pictures from a UNICEF calendar of different families as a catalyst for writing. When she asked students to write about the pictures, many of them sat at their seat doing nothing. She then told them that it was okay to write in Spanish if they wanted or to write in English until they got stuck (and then use Spanish to get unstuck). When she said this, students began writing. One student chose to write in Spanish only; others wrote in English with some Spanish mixed in; one wrote in English only. Loren said she felt that these directions gave her students the liberty to say a lot more in English.

This example shows that the issue of language choice is profoundly linked to self-expression. If our goal is truly to make literacy a vehicle for making meaning and making change, we may need to let go of the notion that expressing oneself in English is the only thing that counts. What's interesting is that by letting go of the need to stress English, we may in fact be providing the most powerful basis for developing literacy in both languages. Our experience has been that once students are able to elaborate their ideas in the first language, their ability to express themselves in the second language is enhanced. The following excerpt from *Talking Shop* illustrates the powerful relationship between giving students choice and control and their language and literacy development (Nash et al., in press).

Loren, the instructor, writes about a lesson in which she had planned to invite students to take pictures and write about their neighborhoods. She intended to model the process by taking pictures of her own neighborhood, and inviting students to do the same. Here she explains what actually happened when she brought her pictures to class.

> I first asked the students what they saw when looking at the pictures as a group. This open approach allowed each student to see and express what she saw in the picture. One student, for example, said, in looking at my picture of a small garden, that this reminded her of her father; that they used to have a garden like this and that her father had died in a garden like this on her birthday. We were all quite taken aback by this sudden and serious comment, but while I was searching around for something comforting and appropriate to say, it seemed as if others had picked up on the idea that these pictures reminded them of gardens back in their countries. They all agreed that my pictures of the fountain and detailed iron work (originally representing my view of the wealthy) looked like parts of Old San Juan and this made them feel homesick. They became quite animated and I could tell they wanted to continue talking about this in Spanish. I let them continue to speak and interrupted only a few times to get clarification for myself, since my Spanish was still very rudimentary. This was the first time they had spoken at length in Spanish in front of me. In the past, they would have done this only with Beatriz, my coteacher, who is Puerto Rican.
>
> I was nervous and unsure of what to do next, since my original lesson plan had evolved into something else. All I knew was that this was where the energy was, and that the writing could come from this. So I asked the students if they wanted to write some of their ideas down. They said yes. I told them to write in whichever language they felt like. Beatriz and I have always given the students the choice to decide which language to write in. In the past when we have done this, Beatriz would read and give feedback to those who wrote in Spanish, and I would do the same for those who wrote in English.
>
> At the end of ten minutes, I asked if people needed more time. Everyone said yes, so we all wrote for another ten minutes. (I feel it is important to give people time limits so they feel secure initially, but I always ask them if they want more time. It is yet another way to create a participatory sense of class management.) I wrote, also, because I was anxious to tell them my interpretation of my pictures. When everyone stopped writing, I suggested that we read our writings aloud. Everyone agreed, but looked a little bashful and uncomfortable. They all had written in Spanish except for Angel (who wrote in English about me, the photographer, who had taken a picture of a Jesus statue). I told them this was no problem and I would ask for clarification when I needed it.
>
> We all read our pieces, laughed, and made comments to each other. It was a very empowering and vulnerable experience for me to be listening to my students read to me in Spanish. I felt vulnerable because I could not be their teacher in the old sense and offer corrections in either Spanish or English. I also felt vulnerable because my Spanish was not great, so I really had to listen and sometimes ask a lot of questions. Yet, I felt empowered because I felt they were now treating me like an equal by not trying to please me by writing in English. The class had reached that level of intimacy one always hopes for; so much so that they were able to discuss with both

interest and understanding one student's struggle to write in Spanish, and why she would rather make mistakes in English than lose face writing in her semi-literate Spanish.

After we had all read our pieces aloud, I admitted to them the surprising turn my lesson had taken and how surprised I was at first that my pictures of my neighborhood looked like places in their home countries. I also felt it was important for me to tell about how I felt listening to them talk and read in Spanish. We all agreed my Spanish had improved over the course of the class, but also that this had been a very special class. (pp. 48-49)

This activity came full circle with the following story written by Maria Rivera (Strohmeyer & McGrail, 1988).

The Park
This picture reminds me when I was 11 years old. This is the park where I played with my sister and niece all day and night.

In this building on the 3rd floor: I lived in these area when I was young. I remember when I wrote some words like the ones that you see in that wall. When I pass through there, I get tears in my eyes, and sometimes when I played there my father always looked at me and called me.

"Mary it is late" and I felt mad and in my mind I wanted to live alone and to do what I wanted.

And now he is dead and I miss him a lot because he took care of me more than my mother. And now I feel sad because my father died on the same day of my birthday.

These two pictures make me think more than you can believe. (p. 23)
Reprinted by permission of Loren McGrail and Beatriz Strohmeyer.

Dealing with Difficult Student Themes and Issues

How can we handle complex, loaded, personal, or explosive issues? The transition from finding a theme to doing something with it isn't always a smooth one. Students may bring up a concern that you as a teacher are uncomfortable with. Or so many themes may come up that you feel overwhelmed. How do you know which to follow up on and which to drop? If a discussion gets hot, how do you bring in a language focus? How do you move day-to-day concerns to the level of social analysis? Teachers face their own issues in trying to determine how best to build curriculum around students' issues.

Again, there are no prescriptions for addressing these questions. Certainly there's no rule that you need to followup on every concern raised by students or that the follow-up must be immediate. Teachers often decide not to pursue an issue when it first comes up because it is an interruption of something important, because they are unsure how to handle it, or because students' energy doesn't sustain itself. The same issue may present itself weeks later, in another context where follow-up does make sense; or the class may never get back to it. Part of the challenge of participatory ESL is knowing when to pursue a theme, when to drop it, and when to come back to it. This is an art that develops over time through experimentation.

The most important thing to remember is that you don't have to decide how to handle these issues by yourself. Both your students and your colleagues are invaluable resources. Making the curriculum development process explicit to students by talking about choices all along the way can lay the groundwork for deciding what to do when particular issues arise. As you read these examples of teacher issues and suggestions for handling them, you may want to compare them to situations you have been in and think about how you did or might respond to them.

If a theme seems overwhelming, focus on a limited aspect of it. Madeline showed us a photo that she wanted to use of an Ethiopian woman and her child, but she was concerned that it might raise the issue of parents' separation from kids. It is such a hard issue to address that it may cause a feeling of hopelessness. In fact, when she showed this picture to her students, it triggered a long and emotional account of one woman's life which was moving and engaging for the others; just the act of telling her story served a powerful function for this woman and the class. At the same time, it is important to find issues that are not so big that students feel helpless—issues where there are possibilities for addressing the problem in some way that may create change. The story about the parking ticket in Chapter 3 is one such example.

If a theme seems too hot or loaded, approach it indirectly. Sometimes removing an issue from its immediate manifestation helps students feel more choice in addressing it. Madeline knew that the political situation in Haiti was very much on her students' minds, but because of deeply-rooted fears of talking about politics, they might be reluctant to raise the issue in class. She approached the subject by introducing a reading on Laos. As students read, an Iranian woman drew a picture of torture in Iran and the discussion moved quickly to the events in Haiti. The class dictated a story about the elections.

If a hot issue arises unexpectedly, focus on language work to defuse the issue. Sometimes a focus on form and language skills can provide distance from the topic, while at the same time providing space for students to decide when to come back to it. This approach allows students to reflect on the issue through a "safe" exercise while satisfying their need to feel that class time is devoted to language instruction. Specifically, when a discussion arises that is hot or confusing for you as a teacher, you can always start by transcribing it (as an LEA story—see p.101). This defuses things, provides a concrete literacy focus, and stalls for time as you figure out what to do next.

If you, as the teacher, aren't clear about how to address a problem, act as a problem-poser rather than a problem-solver. Teachers often feel that they have to have the answers, and steer away from problems that they can't help to solve. Since problem-posing is not designed to solve problems, but rather to explore their causes and enable students to develop their own solutions, teachers don't have to have all the answers. Rather, what's important is facilitating discussion and providing resources without prescribing solutions. In family literacy classes, this dilemma may especially arise around questions of parenting, because of implicit value judgements. No one wants to get into who is or isn't being a good parent. Teachers, in particular, are often in no position to understand the conflicts of raising children in a new culture. At the same time, parents are groping and want direction. It makes sense to look at parenting problems not in terms of do's and don'ts, but in terms of sharing experiences and making resources available. This might mean developing a code to elicit students' concerns about parenting and using these as a way into workshops or experience-sharing rather than acting as an expert on parenting.

If an issue seems too personal, situate it in a broader context. When Ann's student was very preoccupied with a problem at his job (see p. 50), she didn't want to let the issue drop but also didn't want to focus on that person. She removed the issue from the student's particular situation by writing a code about the general problem, inviting other students to bring out related experiences, compare them, and address them together. By finding how individual problems relate to common concerns, the teacher can situate seemingly personal problems to in a broader context.

If you're not sure whether to pursue an issue, involve students in decision-making. Charo felt that it would be important to follow up on some stories about knives in school and safety concerns, but when she suggested activities to develop this theme, students seemed to clam up; their responses shifted to issues of bus safety and communication with teachers. Since one of the goals is to increase student control and involvement, sharing your concerns about what to do and asking students to help decide the direction (providing some choices or leaving it more open-ended) accomplishes two things at once: It takes the heat off the teacher and it increases students' engagement with the process.

If students' analysis of an issue differs from yours, listen, express your perspective and let go of your expectations. Very often in our efforts to link daily concerns to social analysis, we try to draw students toward particular interpretations or understandings of issues. In one case, for example, Andy presented a code about racism as a result of some comments about Blacks that emerged in her class. She wrote two stories, one about two Black men following a woman, the other about a Black man who was beaten up by some White kids while visiting a friend in East Boston. Andy hoped that students would compare the situations, focusing on racism. Instead they talked about ways to be safe (e.g., not walking alone at night). Letting go of control as a teacher may mean that discussions don't always go the way you plan; moreover, this may be a positive sign, rather than a sign of failure. It may mean that a new issue is raised that is more important to them, or that the original issue was really your issue and not theirs. Or it may be that a seed has been planted that students will return to later when they're ready. In any case, teachers need to express their own perspective as coparticipants while at the same time accepting student responses as a reflection of where they are.

Examples of Putting the Principles into Practice

Many of Ann's students were concerned about the impact of the new immigration law so she wrote a story about a woman from El Salvador with no papers who needed a job but was scared to look for one. The story and questions focused on the use of modals. Then there was a true/false opinion quiz about what the woman should do. This led to a heated discussion about alternatives in different situations. Ann followed this with the question, "Who do you think should have the right to live here?" Then students did a role play taking the parts of the President, an employer, and people from other countries. In this situation, Ann used a teacher-written story as a tool to approach a theme of common concern indirectly, framed the issue in a language exercise, elicited rather than imposed alternative ways of addressing the problem, led the discussion to a broader level of analysis, situating individual's concerns in a social context, and involved students in creating their own tool (the sociodrama) as they developed ways of addressing the problem. She went back and forth between a content focus and a language focus, moving toward increasing student participation.

These issues from practice are only the beginning of the story. There are others at every stage of the curriculum development process: How can we link personal concerns to the social context? Is this approach suitable for all cultural groups or only certain ones? What does action mean? We have touched on just a few of the questions arising in participatory ESL/literacy; there are bound to be others. For this reason, what is most important is not so much the particular issues discussed here, but rather the process for dealing with new ones as they arise. The key to participatory curriculum development is having a structure or framework for addressing issues of practice as they arise.

Teacher Sharing: A Framework for Addressing Issues

In our project, the way we dealt with curriculum issues paralleled the process we used with students: We relied on each others' resources, sharing problems, strategies, and materials as equal participants in a common endeavor. Thus, problem-posing became a tool for teachers as well as students. We called this process teacher sharing and tried to schedule it into each weekly meeting. This sharing was an integral part of curriculum development for us. It was a time when teachers talked about what was happening in their classes—describing how a theme emerged, what activities were used to develop it, how it was followed up, and most importantly, concerns that arose out of it (very much following the pattern of questions we asked about your practice on page 38). Instead of describing or reporting on everything everyone was doing, teachers often selected one lesson or issue they were immersed in, sharing why it developed the way it did, possible ideas for what to do next, problems or questions they were thinking about, and unexpected outcomes. If a teacher didn't feel like anything particularly interesting was happening, she might choose not to share anything or talk about why her class was in the doldrums. If there wasn't time for everyone to talk, teachers took turns. If someone felt that an outside resource would be helpful in addressing an issue, we scheduled a workshop or training session on that topic. The best way to get a flavor of how this worked is by reading the minutes of one of our teacher sharing sessions. As you read these minutes, try to identify some of the issues described in this chapter and think about other curriculum issues that are raised.

Madeline's class: M. presented a picture of an Ethiopian woman with her child, a moving picture reflecting sorrow, intimacy. In response to this picture, one of her students got up and acted out the story of her own flight to the U.S.; she told the whole story in English, with dramatic explanations of escaping from the detention center, having no shoes and having to steal them. The whole class was riveted on the story of this woman. This episode raised a number of questions for Madeline: How could she get beyond the individual experience level without detracting from the power of the woman's story? How was this a language/literacy activity? Does this kind of recounting of personal history promote critical thinking? If so, how? If not, how do we get to that level? Others in the group proposed a variety of ways to move beyond this woman's story:

♦ Break the dialogue process into a number of days.

♦ Invite students on the next day to do a follow-up language activity (a language experience story, or comprehension, retelling task centered on wh-questions, or small group writing activities about the story).

♦ Move from a language activity to generalizing questions:

♦ Why did you leave your country? How did you leave?

♦ Why do so many people from your country come to the U.S.?

♦ If the students pursue the issue of being separated from children, as questions like, "How can you continue to support your children from far away?"

Loren's class: In response to the question about whether the dialogue process itself is too invasive, and what to do if students balk at discussing issues, Loren suggested making the language focus of the lesson more explicit. She described how she uses codes for grammar work to addresss the students' and teachers' desire for structured language exercises.

♦ Scramble lines of the dialogue on the board. Ask students context questions: How many people are talking? What nationality are they? Where is this taking place? Someone suggested also asking: How do you know?

♦ Ask students to reconstruct the dialogue so that it makes sense.

♦ Discuss the reconstructed dialogue in terms of vocabulary, and structures, asking: Is there anything new here?

- Write the questions for discussion on cards and divide them into piles with one question from each of the five levels in each pile. In groups of three, students discuss their pile: one person asks questions, one responds and one takes notes.
- Report back: students read and discuss each others' responses.

At first students continued to give answers that they thought Loren wanted—the answers still felt canned. As Loren proceeded through the steps with a language focus and breaking the lesson down into parts (using larger print) students began for the first time to respond in terms of the content of the issue: paradoxically, because the content is loaded, the language focus allows students the security to begin to get at the content.

Charo's class: In the middle of the unit dealing with negative stereotypes about homelands, a woman came into class and said she couldn't continue class because one of her kids had been stabbed. This prompted an outpouring of stories about violence in the schools: knives in the bathroom, 12-year-olds bringing knives to school for self-defense, etc. This outburst raised many questions for Charo: How should she handle this in terms of teaching? Should she try to get back on target with the homelands project or pursue the concerns about violence? Is this too big a subject to take on? Is this an interruption? If the class does pursue the violence theme, what can they do about it?

The first question seemed to be whether to do anything at all about the theme or get back to the homelands project. Andy suggested that Charo bring this question back to the students themselves to see what they wanted to do. We discussed what the class might do in terms of literacy work and action if they decided to pursue the violence issue.

- Start by extending the discussion to reasons for the violence (the social context) and alternative approaches to dealing with violence (eg. discussing things like the proposed body searches); talk about what parents can do (possible actions and their consequences).
- Document in testimonial form the experiences of immigrant parents with violence in the schools (e.g., language experience stories/oral histories/ student writing).
- Use this documentation as a possible basis for action, e.g., going to the media (letters to the editor, news releases, pamphlets/interview with local columnist).
- Write photo stories to support the documentation.
- Participate in parent-teacher meetings and other collaborations.

Ann's class: Ann presented a story about loneliness that one of her students had written. She did this as a result of another discussion about whether or not to talk about students' own lives in class: some had felt that it was a waste of time, but the conclusion they came to was that student stories should be mixed with other activities, written up and presented as language activities with the student's permission. The loneliness story was one such activity. It prompted discussion about how students can deal with loneliness in a new country, as well as an interesting side discussion about whether going to English class is the same as learning English!

---

7 Action: Using Literacy to Make Change

The bottom line in a participatory approach is *action*—using literacy to address real issues and to make changes in the social context through collective effort. As Wallerstein (1983) says,

> Critical thinking begins when people make the connections between their individual lives and social conditions. It ends one step beyond perception—toward the action people take to regain control over social structures detrimental to their lives. (p. 16)

What differentiates action in a participatory perspective from traditional approaches oriented toward individual outcomes is that it is linked to reflection and to social transformation. It encompasses not just personal changes in behaviors, language, or competencies, but also changes in consciousness about the relation between the individual and society.

> Freirean social action extends beyond community activity for activity's sake. The goal of Freirean action is to promote justice, and to change power relationships which would give people a greater voice in policy development and community decision-making. [Further], as a result of praxis (or reflections on the actions), transformation is also expected within the internal structure of the group working on social change and within individuals. (Wallerstein, 1991, pp. 16-17)

Your Practice...

1. **Write down some changes that students made in their lives as a result of your classes**
   ♦ Did they become involved in any community activities, find work, make changes in their families, participate in events, anything else?

2. **After noting these changes, compare your lists:**
   ♦ What kinds of changes did you count?
   ♦ What did you see as important?
   ♦ Did your lists include any kinds of social action?

Our Practice...

Initially, we interpreted Freire's and Wallerstein's concepts of action to mean that the outcome of classroom interaction around each issue had to be some form of concrete, visible social change outside the classroom—that addressing an issue didn't "count" if it wasn't followed by an immediate attempt to transform conditions in students' lives. But given this analysis, we had to ask ourselves whether our practice really achieved this goal. As themes developed in our classes, they led in many directions, few of which were organized attempts to make direct changes outside the classroom. Where were the examples of students fighting for better housing conditions after a unit on housing, resisting discrimination after a unit on work, or participating in parents' groups after a unit on schooling? Measuring our practice by this narrow standard, it seemed that instances of action were few and far between.

Yet clearly, our students were making changes, both individually and collectively. Rosa went to community college; Hilda became more active in her school PTA; Angel had many of his writings published and read his work publicly at several events; Maria joined a Hispanic parents' advocacy group; Quisqueya's daughter received a merit award in school after almost having been kept back; and Nilsa joined a softball team. The stories go on.

Classes made internal changes, improving attendance, learning to work cooperatively, helping each other with problems. Roles changed to the point where students felt comfortable telling the teacher they were tired of an activity, refused to go on with it, and suggested something else instead. For some, action took the form of choosing to write in their own language as an affirmation of identity; for others, it meant gaining the confidence to write in English without fear of mistakes. In one site, a class developed guidelines for discussing personal issues and strategies for increasing safety in coming to class; in another, classes discussed criteria for hiring new teachers, presenting their ideas at center-wide meetings to determine hiring criteria and procedures. Classes used literacy to provide support in their communities. One group of mothers wrote letters of advice to pregnant teenagers in another city; another class developed a housing project newsletter. Whole classes participated in public hearings about ESL services and funding; individual students got up and testified before hundreds of people at these public meetings. Students discussed "English-only" legislation and went as a group to hearings at the State House. They wrote letters to the Governor about cuts in services and letters to the editor about cases of discrimination.

What we learned from all this is that change takes many forms, both inside and outside the classroom. Rather than being packaged only in discrete actions, it is often a nonlinear, nonsequential process that develops unevenly. As such, action may not, as we originally thought, be the direct result of particular curriculum units; rather, it may be the result of invisible changes—the cumulative building of confidence, validation of experience, and reflection on context. Very often it takes months or even years of germination before students are ready to move outside the classroom with their actions. During this time, the changing social relations within the classroom, the critical examination of day to day reality, and the development of language and literacy are all functioning as a kind of rehearsal for external action. Thus, there is an interaction between external actions and changes in the internal dynamic of the group.

Examples

A closer examination of the examples of Maria, the student who became a member of the Hispanic parents' advocacy group, and Nilsa, who joined a softball team, illuminates how we came to reinterpret the meaning of action. Maria was a student in one of Loren's classes for over a year. During this time, the class did extensive work on issues of community, schooling, and bilingualism. Although she had strong concerns about the schooling of Hispanic children in Boston, Maria aired them primarily in class, but did little about them outside of class. However, shortly after the class ended, when the Hispanic Parent Association was formed to fight for school reform, she was one of the first parents to join. She attended meetings with the superintendent, press conferences, and organizational meetings and actively tried to recruit others. When the time was right for her, and the external conditions conducive, she was able to act on ideas that had been developing over time. Her participation didn't result from a particular lesson or code, but from many months of dialogue, and from the support and confidence she gained from her class.

The second example taught us that an action doesn't need to take an explicitly political form to signify change in students' relation to the social context of their lives; it may take a form completely different from anything we anticipated. In this case, students in one of Charo's classes were discussing a picture of a woman surrounded by cooking, housework, and childcare responsibilities. This led to a discussion of what motherhood means. Students listed all they people they are, using the format "Women are _____" (mothers, cooks, etc.). Someone said, "Women are persons" and the conversation turned toward individuals' desires and goals; students talked about what they wanted to do for themselves and about obstacles in pursuing their own interests. Nilsa talked about the fact that she never had time for herself, to do what she wanted to do for her own enjoyment and development. The group talked about why—that maybe her husband didn't support her in this. A few weeks later, Nilsa came to class and announced that she had joined a women's softball team! Through the discussion and support of the class, she had decided to assert her desire to do this in her family and had done it. Even though it was an individual action, it was possible because of what had happened in class.

These examples illustrate two very different routes toward action. In one case, the action was a direct outgrowth of a particular lesson; in the other, the cause-effect relationship was much less clear or direct. What we don't want to imply is that one lesson or code *should* lead to action.

A common reaction as students consider taking action is fear. Often students are afraid of making waves because they are immigrants and, in some cases, undocumented. They don't want to do anything to draw attention to themselves or to jeopardize their status here. Clearly, it is impossible to consider action without considering its consequences, and students may well know better than we do what is or isn't dangerous for them. In some cases, however, this fear immobilizes students, making them unable even to consider ways of improving the conditions in their lives. Our role in this is not to impose our own views of what students should or shouldn't do, but rather to make the classroom a safe place to consider the possibilities and consequences. Of course, legal status is an extremely delicate subject, which must be handled with great care; but, precisely because it is so loaded, it is important to recognize and explore its ramifications with students. Our experience has been that students are eager for information and a chance to talk about legal status if it is broached sensitively.

First, raising the issue in a depersonalized way (through stories about other people, in the third person) helps to make it safer; Unit V, Lesson 1 of *ESL for Action* (Auerbach & Wallerstein, 1987) provide examples of how to do this. Another way of doing this is by presenting a news story or external event (like the changes in the immigration law) to introduce the topic in a context removed from personal situations.

Second, providing legal information about the rights of the foreign-born gives students a sense of their protections (or lack of protection); discussion of this information should be contextualized in analysis of the strengths and the limits of legal strategies. Inviting outside speakers is not only a way to deal with questions beyond the teacher's knowledge, but also puts students in contact with community resources.

Third, and most importantly, is presenting examples of success stories—news articles or personal accounts of cases where immigrants acted successfully to make change. In Boston, for example, Local 26 of the Hotel and Restaurant Workers Union has achieved a number of highly publicized victories—one in which room cleaners resisted changes in their working conditions, another in which the union won a court case against a landlord who was recruiting immigrant tenants, charging them high rents and refusing to make repairs because, as he said, "they pay their rent without arguing." Examples like these not only show that change is possible but provide rich lessons in how to go about the process.

I'll Get Fired!

A related issue is students' legitimate concern about individual consequences to their actions. They may feel that if they take a stand (e.g., write a letter, challenge a landlord or boss), they might be singled out for some form of retribution—they could lose their job, get evicted, harassed, or investigated. For example, some students were reluctant to sign the letter about police discrimination, fearing that they would be punished somehow for their actions.

In addressing this concern, it is important that the teacher not impose counterarguments, but rather draw out the divergence of perspectives from the group. Certainly, urging students to take individual actions with no built-in protection would be irresponsible. More importantly, the real learning comes when students see that their collective resources are their strength. Our experience has been that they very often arrive at the understanding through dialogue that there is both power and safety in numbers. This discussion is as important as whatever decision is reached. The key is on the one hand creating a forum for examining possibilities together and on the other trusting the students to do what they are comfortable with. In the case of the letter to the editor, students went through a long debate about whether to sign it, with several students refusing to do so, but in the end, everyone signed it anyway.

Nothing Ever Changes Anyway!

Fatalism, cynicism, and skepticism are prevalent among students. Many feel that their situations are inevitable, or that the world will always be the way it is. Addressing this concern, which is after all the ultimate goal of participatory education, is an ongoing process. Again, showing is more powerful than telling. This can be done by a combination of focusing on finite issues with possible immediate strategies, introducing success stories, conducting social analysis, and relying on group resources.

But what happens when a group takes the step toward action and the action fails to achieve the desired outcome? For example, after students went through the long process of formulating a letter about police discrimination (the many stages of drafting, the decision about where to send it, the decision about whether to sign individual names, etc.), and finally sent it to a citywide newspaper, it never was published. Clearly, seeing the letter in print or getting a response would have been a happier ending. However, it is important to remember that this is a problem-posing process, not a problem-solving process. It is inevitable that some actions will meet with success and others won't. The analysis that the action is embedded in is more important than its actual result. "Failures" cease to be problematic if the teacher doesn't set the students up to expect positive results for each action, but rather uses the outcome to deepen the understanding of the social context. The class can analyze why the action got the response it did, what the response shows about the institutions it was directed toward, and what else they might have done or could do in the future. Even when an action meets with students' expectations, it may raise new issues (e.g., once parents met with the superintendent, they had to figure out how to deal with his response). This kind of evaluation is an essential component of the critical thinking—action—critical thinking cycle.

It's Not My Issue!

Often students are reluctant to become involved in actions that don't directly affect them. They may not want to be bothered, not see the importance or relevance of the action, or just be uninterested. A case in point was the issue of a school closing in the neighborhood of one of our sites. When one student brought a petition to class for others to sign, several class members felt the issue didn't concern them because they didn't have children at the school. Others argued that the school closing would increase the drop-out rate, affecting neighborhood safety for everyone; that if this happened in one school, it could happen in another; and that a united community effort would increase the chances of a successful campaign. In the end, most of the students signed (and, incidentally, because of broad-based community resistance that this discussion was part of, the school remained open). Again, the discussion process enabled the various arguments to be aired so students could arrive at their own conclusions.

Another instance occurred in Ann's class around the time of the changes in the immigration laws; there was a citywide hearing and demonstration that provided an external focus for discussing students' concerns. However, this was an issue that affected students differently, because some were citizens already (e.g., Puerto Ricans), some were refugees, some were legal immigrants, and others were undocumented. The following excerpt from our minutes shows how the class addressed these issues.

> Ann started with a true/false questionnaire with attitude questions like "If there were a march about the new immigration law, no one would come" to get at people's ideas, fears and opinions about participation. This brought out discussion about all the reasons people might not participate—time, family commitments, fear. Many students said

they are afraid of being caught right there at a march. One student had participated in various kinds of actions and was able to talk about her experiences; she said that it's not like it is in home countries where people are grabbed at events. But people's fears are real and we can't offer them assurances that nothing will happen. Ann then brought in a reading about a community coming together to help during the 1930's as a example. We also suggested asking students (like the woman who did participate actively), "What makes people to decide to participate?" which might help them to think about whether and under what conditions it's worth it to them to take action.

We also talked about how to explore the relevance of the issue for people not directly affected by the laws. Some suggestions were:

• Asking students "What did you do to get here?" (outlining the different steps for each group) as a way to develop some understanding and empathy for the different situations of immigrants, refugees, Puerto Ricans, etc. and to find the common ground.

• Using quotes from the newspaper about possible effects of the new laws as catalysts.

• Asking how the new law will affect everyone's possibilities and work situations as well as children's possibilities. Even if students aren't working themselves, many have teenage children whose chances for finding work may be affected.

In each of the above examples of issues that arise in considering and taking action, the central point is that the process is as important as the outcome. We have found that if the teacher draws out the diversity of experience and creates an atmosphere where students can express their perspectives openly, the resources of the group are often rich enough to address the concerns outlined here. More importantly, the dialogue leading up to and following decisions to take action determine students' ability to extend critical thinking to new domains. Going through the steps of the dialogue process, learning to analyze the social context, and relying on group resources are the real benefits of participatory education.

Redefining Action

Looking at these accumulated experiences over time, we began to realize that it was not so much our practice, but our initial concept of action that was flawed. Just as we couldn't predetermine curriculum content, we couldn't predetermine the forms action should take. Students changed at their own rates, when they were ready, and in terms of their own needs. Sometimes these changes were individual, internal, and invisible; sometimes they were collective, external and explicit.

An important aspect of this was realizing that the context and composition of the class shapes the possibilities for action. If students come from many parts of the city, different backgrounds, or different employment situations, they don't have these areas of their lives in common, so group action around issues arising from them is less possible or likely. For these groups, action may take place primarily inside the classroom, in terms of changes in classroom dynamics and language and literacy accomplishments (publishing writing, producing photostories, etc.).

While we felt the lack of an external organizational base as a constraint on certain kinds of action, it became clear that there were a wealth of forms that action could take, and, to be genuinely participatory, we couldn't direct students only toward those outcomes that fit with our preconceptions. Rather, we had to challenge students to link what was happening in class to their lives outside of class and validate changes as they took place. In addition, we had to understand that the consequences of what happens in class don't always take place during the teaching cycle itself and that, in fact, we may never see the actions that result from our work.

Finally, we had to realize that group actions don't fall from the sky, with whole groups deciding to do something at once, but rather that they often start with one or two people taking the initiative, having a success which others hear about and begin to network around. With these realizations in mind, we moved toward an expanded concept of action that included the following forms:

Using Literacy to Make Change

Examples	Form of Action
Individual, Personal internal	♦ gains in self confidence ♦ affective change
external	♦ joining softball team ♦ becoming active in community/school organizations
literacy-related	♦ publishing writing ♦ reading work at public events ♦ changing uses of literacy in everyday life ♦ affirming identity through use of first language
In Class	♦ determining curriculum content ♦ asserting preference for activities ♦ addressing issues of classroom dynamics (attendance, uneven participation, use of L1 vs. L2, handling of personal information) ♦ rehearsing for outside action ♦ class publications or productions (photo stories, anthologies of student writings)
In Site	♦ participating in evaluation/decision-making ♦ participating in hiring ♦ participating in advocacy activities
In Family	♦ diversifying literacy uses ♦ changing dynamics around literacy (becoming independent of children, gaining confidence in helping chidren) ♦ gaining pride in first language/culture ♦ reinforcing home culture and use of L1
In Relation to School	♦ participating in school events ♦ advocating for child/children
In Relation to Immediate Community	♦ joining community organizations or activities (parents' group, action to keep school open) ♦ taking on new responsibilities (helping others with literacy tasks dealing with bureaucracy, etc.) ♦ strengthening community ties (e.g., through newsletter, networking)
In Broader Community	♦ participating in funding hearings ♦ participating in demonstrations on bilingual education ♦ writing letters to the editor ♦ writing letters to/petitioning officials

A collage of actions that our students participated in:

28 THE BOSTON GLOBE THURSDAY, DECEMBER 22, 1988

Hispanic parents demand talks with Wilson

By Gus Martins
Contributing Reporter

A group of Hispanic parents, united under a new citywide organization, yesterday demanded that Superintendent of Schools ... S. Wilson resume discus-... how to de-

The group also protested a comment by Wilson in the Sunday New York Times two weeks ago calling it "discriminatory" to form special programs or initiatives to lower the dropout rate among Hispanics.

At a news conference at School Department headquarters on Court Street, group members said ... administrators ... needed

---

Publisher, mayor launch literacy fund to help all residents share city's boom

By David Arnold
Globe Staff

The mayor and a newspaper publisher put the polish on yesterday's kickoff for a major public-private partnership aimed at fighting adult illiteracy, but the quiet words from three shy and once-illiterate residents gave the event its guts.

Mayor Flynn and William O. Taylor, publisher of The Boston Globe, launched the Adult Literacy Fund Inc., which aims to raise $5 million in the next five years to augment existing community literacy programs.

"One in eight American families are functionally illiterate," Taylor told an estimated 75 people packed shoulder-to-shoulder in a conference room in the Cardinal Cushing Center on Washington Street. Members of these families not only are unable to read a newspaper, Taylor said, but they cannot even read an election ballot ...ment pla...

lion at work by the end of 1989. Fund-raising will target sources not already supporting the 30 existing community-based adult programs, which serve fewer than 4 percent of those estimated to be in need. Yesterday's announcement comes on the heels of the state release Monday of $8 million, budgeted last year to fund literacy programs across the state for the second half of the current fiscal year.

The literacy fund will bolster community programs by providing money for needs such as additional teachers, better salaries and ch... di... Community programs obs... fit from the fund r fu... WAITT House in Roxb... ac... Cardinal Cushing Cen... the Charlestown Com...n h... School, represented y...ld... by students Theresa ...sh... Maria Rivera and Hele...co... fano respectively. ...d...

To a hushed audien...

During the South... Wilson's first with the rece... formed Hispanic Parent Association, he said his staff will begin translating a summary of the controversial plan today.

"How can you have parent involvement when you don't translate these important documents?" demanded Javier Colon, attorney for the association.

Sta... Dorchester) s... tion saying. ...ting an edu... are clear. T... studied, the Althoug... meet with lv when i...

HISPANIC PARENTS MOBILIZE IN BOSTON

Saying a 'Pattern of Neglect' Has Led to Dropouts, They Urge School Programs

By SUSAN DIESENHOUSE
Special to The New York Times

BOSTON, Dec. 8 — Accusing the Boston schools of "a pattern of neglect," a group of parents has mobilized to press officials to give special attention to Hispanic students not in bilingual education programs.

Most Hispanic children here speak English and thus are not enrolled in such programs, and school officials say they have a higher dropout rate than those who are. Hispanic children over all have the city's highest dropout rate.

The Hispanic Parents Association, a group of about two dozen members that met for the first time last night, says a dropout prevention program needs to be designed especially for students who are not in bilingual programs.

The parents say these ...h...n ...

THE NEW YORK TIMES, SUNDAY, DECEMBER 11, 1988

Photo: Margarita Henriquez

Making Meaning, Making Change ♦ 107

8 Evaluation: What Counts as Progress?

The final question we need to consider in curriculum development is "What does it all add up to?" or, more accurately, "How do we determine what it adds up to?" Unfortunately, the question of evaluating progress is one of the most problematic and neglected in adult literacy. Currently, a kind of tug of war exists between funders/administrators and practitioners/educators over what counts as success and how to measure it. The former often insist on concrete, quantifiable, and objective indications of progress, often taking numerical form, while the latter resist or disagree with the forms of evaluation demanded of them. However, because continued funding depends on compliance with funders' mandates, a charade ensues, with teachers going through the motions to make their numbers look good (it is not uncommon for teachers to admit privately to fudging their paperwork to show progress) while never having the time or energy to develop other forms of evaluation that would more genuinely reflect their perspectives on adult learning.

This was an issue that we struggled with throughout the life of our project: How could we document what students were actually learning in a way that corresponded to our philosophy, and, at the same time, satisfy demands for accountability? We were in the fortunate position of having both the time and the staff development framework to allow us to explore this question, try different approaches suggested by others, and attempt to develop our own responses. In this chapter, we will present an overview and critique of current approaches, trace our own thinking on evaluation, and suggest some specific assessment and evaluation forms and procedures that are congruent with participatory adult literacy; much of what is proposed here draws heavily on the work of others (Balliro, 1989; Lytle, 1988; Hemmingdinger, 1988.) This is by no means a fully developed, definitive alternative evaluation scheme, but rather a proposal for a process that needs to be refined through collective practice and reflection by adult educators in different contexts.

Your Practice...

Again, we'd like to start by asking you to reflect on your past experience or current practice, discussing your responses if you are working with a group.

1. *What/who* gets evaluated in your program?
♦ students (student learning/progress)?
♦ teachers (teacher effectiveness)?
♦ administrators (administrator effectiveness)?
♦ curriculum content?
♦ overall program design?
♦ course materials/texts?
♦ assessment instruments/evaluation procedures?
♦ program impact in the community?
♦ other?

2. *When* are assessment and evaluation conducted?
♦ before instruction?
♦ after instruction?
♦ ongoing?

3. *Who* does the evaluating?
♦ students?
♦ teachers?
♦ support staff (e.g., counselors)?
♦ administrators?

- external evaluators?
- other?

4. *How* is student assessment conducted?
- oral interviews?
- tests? (what kind?—standardized? program-developed?)
- performance standards (measures of competencies)?
- collections of student work (writing samples)?
- observation of classroom interactions?
- self-report?
- ongoing documentation (teacher reports)?
- other?

5. *What counts* as progress?
- reading level gains?
- test scores?
- effective gains in self-confidence.?
- ability to use language/literacy outside the class?
- ability to make changes (person/classroom/community)?
- other?

6. *Who* gets the results/findings from assessment/evaluation?
- students?
- teachers?
- program administrators?
- funders?
- other?

7. *How* are the results/findings of assessment/evaluation used?
- for placement and promotion?
- to inform curriculum development?
- to provide feedback to students on their own learning?
- to provide information to funders?
- to inform curriculum design?
- other?

8. What do you like about your current assessment/evaluation system?

9. What do you dislike about it? How would you change it if you could?

10. Why do you think it is set up as it is? Whose interests does it serve?

What Characterizes the Predominant Model of Evaluation?

When Balliro (1989) surveyed teachers, administrators, and funders of adult ESL programs in New England, she found a picture of concern for accountability on the one hand, and dissatisfaction with existing assessment procedures on the other. Because of what she calls "demands for standardized accountability of progress," (p.14) most programs assessed students in terms of externally defined criteria: either performance standards like those of the MELT (Mainstream English Language Training) curriculum, standardized tests, or home-grown tests.

Although the sample in Balliro's study was small, it reflects the current paradigm for ESL literacy assessment nationally, a paradigm that can be characterized as stressing "accountability through quantification." The bottom line for program, curriculum, and teacher evaluation is the ability to show student progress through numbers. Achievement is based on performance on uniform, objective measures; many states mandate the use of specific standardized tests like the TABE (Tests of Adult Basic Education), the ABLE (Adult Basic Learning Examination), the BEST (Basic English Skills Test), or CASAS (California Adult Student Assessment System). These tests often focus on decontextualized word recognition, or on sentence or paragraph comprehension skills, using paper and pencil formats with multiple choice or fill-in-the blank questions. Even with performance standards, like those of MELT, or program-designed tests, outcomes are strictly regulated in terms of measurability (test scores, reading levels, performance standards, numbers of students promoted or placed). Funding is contingent on attaining predefined acceptable outcomes; some programs are even paid on a head count basis for those students actually placed in jobs.

Assessment is usually done on a pretest/posttest basis. Intake tests, often administered by support staff, are used for placement but not to inform instruction or curriculum development (teachers either don't see the results or see only the scores). As one teacher (cited by Balliro) said, "There's no relationship between what's tested initially and what's taught in class." (p.14) Further, test results are rarely shared with students. Ongoing informal assessments by teachers don't usually count for program evaluation purposes. Exit tests, according to Balliro (1989), are used "to place students..., to provide information for the next teacher..., or to determine a grade" (p.18) but rarely to inform students about the development of their own learning.

What's Wrong with this Model?

Teachers' reservations about this paradigm are pervasive. The most common complaint is that instruction suffers because of paper-work demands: Time that could be spent on preparation or teaching instead is taken up by testing and filling in forms. However, as the following pages indicate, critiques go far deeper than these logistical issues and, increasingly, have come not just from the grass roots, but from mainstream professional organizations and educators. The Delegates Assembly of the International Reading Association, for example, adopted the following resolution in 1988:

> Reading assessment must reflect advances in the understanding of the reading process. As teachers of literacy we are concerned that instructional decisions are too often made from assessments which define reading as a sequence of discrete skills that students must master to become readers. Such assessments foster inappropriate instruction. (p.1)

A growing body of research supports the view that the teacher, rather than the test, is the "critical evaluation instrument" (Johnston, 1989). In adult ESL literacy, as well, there are increasing calls for changes in existing assessment practices; perhaps the single most concise statement of the rationale for these changes and the features of an alternative model can be found in Lytle's article in *Focus on Basics* (1988).

Testing is not appropriate or feasible for early literacy learners. One of the teachers Balliro interviewed said that she realized the futility of using the BEST test (supposedly designed for low literate ESL students) because her students "couldn't even hold it right." (p.15) Another educator claims that 40% of those who qualify for the amnesty ESL classes don't even place on the entry tests because their levels are so low. For these students, testing only leads to a sense of frustration and inadequacy.

Funders' demands lead to "creaming." Often, programs are forced to accept only those students who are proficient enough to make short-term gains on tests or to be quickly placed in jobs because these are the measures that determine continued funding. This means that the lowest level students are excluded from services because it takes longer for them to show progress on tests or become ready for employment.

The testing process itself is intimidating and demeaning. Because of prior negative experiences, students may feel uncomfortable about taking tests. For many adults, testing triggers associations with childhood failures or with being judged on the basis of what they can't do rather than on what they can do. It is stressful and anxiety-provoking. Dugan, Skinner, and Tirone (1987) claim that tests like the TABE, adapted from tests for middle-class children, are inappropriate for adults: Questions about farm animals and birds in the park are irrelevant and may be perceived as condescending.

To frame results in terms of grade levels is destructive. Schema research suggests that reading performance varies according to task, context, content, and purpose. Grade-level descriptors don't capture this variability, yet they continue to be used to indicate proficiency. This sends a negative message: "When...adults are informed that their performance is comparable to second or third graders, much more is being communicated than an objective description of ability" (Lytle, 1988, p. 2).

The concept and content of standardized testing are culture-specific. Dugan et al. (1987) found that even for highly literate college ESL graduates, the concept of standardized tests was culturally unfamiliar. For those with little prior education, the process of testing may be even more alien. Further, test content often presupposes culture-specific knowledge and vocabulary, which, as schema research indicates, immediately biases the tests against those from other cultures. As Dugan et al. (1987) say, to subject ESL students to a test like the TABE, "which is first alien to their previous experience and second does not reflect their abilities, is unconscionable and objectionable" (p.4).

The claim for objectivity in testing is misleading. One of the primary arguments for the use of standardized tests—that they are objective—has been widely challenged. Johnston (in press) argues that evaluation of human learning is always, by definition, interpretive. Both the processes we are examining and the tools for examining them are cultural in nature and situated in a social context; hence, the notion of a "pure" measure of reading ability is fraught with problems. Dugan et al.'s (1987) analysis of the TABE debunks the myth of its objectivity as an instrument for assessing adult ESL.

Existing tests measure the wrong things. Because it is easier to tabulate discrete answers, tests focus on subskills like letter and word recognition (assessed by the reading of isolated word lists), and the ability to recall specific facts and perform tasks with predetermined outcomes, which promotes a reductionist view of literacy. As Goodman (cited in Berglund, 1989/90) says, research points to a "rejection of the concept of teaching parts, but we are continually pushed to use tests that focus on parts"(p. 34).

Existing tests fail to measure the right things. Overemphasis on countable skills leads to the neglect of other important aspects of literacy like critical thinking, creativity, and real-world literacy usage, which are less amenable to measurement. Dugan et al. (1987) claim that the test-taking conditions themselves differ from real-world contexts for literacy use where meaning can be negotiated and literacy is a social activity. Tests fail to reveal the ways that adult learners use literacy in daily life; students are rarely asked to read and respond to whole passages, to create meaning through writing, or to indicate how their attitudes and usage of literacy in daily life changed as a result of instruction (Lytle, Marmor, & Penner, 1986).

Tests don't provide information about affective and metacognitive factors in literacy acquisition. The impact of literacy on students' family life, personal growth, effectiveness at work, or ability to make changes in their lives isn't reflected by test scores, although these effects are among the most important from students' perspectives (see Lytle et al., 1986). Although research indicates that factors like learners' internalized model of the reading process, awareness of their own reading strategies, motivation, and ability to utilize prior knowledge and identify text structure are key in proficient reading, none of these is assessed by standardized tests. Because tests focus on product rather than process, they have little explanatory power: The reasons that underly the test results are obscured and neglected.

Performance-based assessment and competency checklists avoid some of these pitfalls but perpetuate others. Measures such as competency tests of performance on real-life tasks are a step forward from traditional tests, but still have shortcomings (see Auerbach, 1986). Purposes continue to be determined externally and measured quantitatively without regard to affective or metacognitive factors; content is often still reductionist in its focus on isolated competencies or behaviors. Assessment goals continue to shape instruction; as one of the teachers in Balliro's study said, "We didn't want a competency checklist, either, because it predetermines what is taught." (p.15) Most importantly, the emphasis on teaching life skills for functioning in the society as it exists carries an implicit agenda of uncritical acceptance of the status quo which serves to perpetuate existing social relations.

Testing shapes teaching. Despite teachers' best intentions, the tail wags the dog; if program evaluation is based on test performance, curricula are inevitably geared toward teaching to the tests. Tests generally measure subskills, so this is what gets taught. Balliro's (1989) accounts of teachers spending class time rehearsing students for test items are all too familiar to ESL teachers, as is her claim that "assessment often determines the content of instruction and is often contradictory to assumptions we have about literacy and language acquisition" (p.2).

Testing and teaching-to-tests reinforce a bottom-up view of literacy. The subskills test-oriented instruction may reinforce "distorted notions that students [have] about what is involved in learning to read and write, i.e., that reading is sounding out words and writing is handwriting" (Lytle et al., 1986, p. 20). Even when literacy is taught holistically, if the tests contain decontextualized word lists or paragraphs with multiple choice questions, the instructional message is undermined.

The testing model conflicts with a student-centered model of adult learning. An important aspect of adult learning is student control and involvement in determining the goals, objectives, and content of learning; yet the test-oriented paradigm removes control from students.

> This view of evaluation puts the power and the responsibility for the program outcomes in the hands of the educators and leaves the learner as yet another object in the learning enterprise, one which is done to and done for rather than done with. (Sauvé, 1987, p. 56)

Students neither participate in assessing their own learning, nor use results for their own purposes.

Our Practice...   Although the critique of the testing paradigm has been clearly articulated, there is as yet no agreement on the particular forms that alternatives should take. Lytle (1988) argues that what's needed is "program-based practitioner research conducted simultaneously in many sites"(p. 4). This is a period of experimentation which, as in any paradigm shift, precedes broad acceptance of a new model. We saw our work as part of this exploratory shift and set ourselves the task of finding alternatives.

The first questions we faced were "Who is assessment for?" and "What is its purpose?" We started with the understanding that assessment must correspond to program philosophy and goals, since, as Lytle et al. (1986) said, "Assessment procedures embody and thus convey particular concepts about literacy"(p. 22). We wanted assessment to serve curriculum development rather than vice versa and hence, as Andy Nash (1989) said, we sought to

> find or create new assessment tools that: 1.) provide more useful information for teachers and students; and 2.) include students in the process of setting goals and evaluating their own progress toward those goals. (p. 1)

The next question we faced was, "What counts as progress?" Because program goals emphasized using literacy to make changes both individually and collectively, indications of progress had to go beyond one-shot test or competency performance to include ongoing changes in literacy use and everyday life both inside and outside the classroom. These may include changes in self-concept, attitudes, or conceptions of literacy, diversification of reading and writing practices in everyday life, actions resulting from program participation as well as totally unexpected, unpredictable changes. Many of these are subjective, intangible changes that aren't amenable to quantification; *what really counts can't be counted.*

This led us to the question, "How can these kinds of progress be assessed?" Since the goal of instruction is related to the significance of literacy in everyday life, we felt that the starting point had to be some kind of exploration of what students were already doing with literacy, where and how they used it, how they conceptualized it, and what changes they wanted to make. Our thinking here was influenced by Lytle et al. (1986), who had developed a two-hour intake interview for ABE students, designed to "emphasize competence, process and use rather than deficiency and to explore the different roles that literacy plays in the lives of different people" (p. 30). The interview investigated students' life circumstances, educational and employment backgrounds, social networks, community involvement, reasons for seeking further education, ways they use literacy, and conceptions about it. Literacy was assessed by giving students a range of contextualized tasks to choose from (reading real-world materials and passages written by other literacy students).

Although we liked many aspects of this approach, we questioned the feasibility of detailed individual interviews with students whose English was minimal and were concerned that interviews would be too time consuming and cumbersome. Further, we were hesitant about asking personal questions, fearing the process might seem intrusive and reinforce a power differential between interviewer and interviewee. Most importantly, we wanted to ensure that assessment contribute to, rather than detract from or interfere with instruction. We came up with an initial plan to develop three kinds of assessment tools designed as in-class activities for the beginning and end of each cycle: (a) *a series of activities and questions* designed to get at the kind of information in Lytle's intake interview, but geared toward classes as a whole rather than toward individual students; (b) *a collection of thematically organized readings* with highly relevant content selected both from student writings and published sources at a range of levels of difficulty from which students could choose; (c) *a set of pictures about learning situations to catalyze writing* which would become the basis for exploring student conceptions about education as well as provide writing samples. Our original idea was that we would begin and end each cycle with the same activities, assessing how students' reading, writing, and ideas about education changed.

As soon as we started to develop and use these activities, however, it became clear that it was unrealistic to view them as pre- and post-cycle tools. Just doing the activities (e.g., writing about the learning pictures) became an extended instructional unit in itself, sometimes taking weeks; the process of collecting appropriate readings took months, and teachers wanted to use the collection as a teaching resource rather than limit its use to assessment. Further, each group of students responded differently. In some cases, students became very involved, and in others, they saw the activity as an interruption of what they were already doing. In short, our notion of a uniform set of activities to be used with all classes at the beginning and end of each cycle did not correspond to the reality of the teaching situations; the separation between assessment and instruction seemed artificial.

At the same time that we were trying to develop these formal tools as a group, some interesting things were happening informally in the classrooms. Loren's students were writing dialogue journals and collecting other writings in portfolios; Andy developed a newsletter for reporting on ongoing classroom activities; Madeline was keeping her own journal of accounts of classroom activities; Charo's class began posted accomplishments lists; at Ann's site, students were participating in evaluations of their own learning, of their teachers, and of the program. Each site was developing evaluation processes that emerged from its particular context. It became clear that rather than strive to find one uniform tool to fit all classes, we needed to find a range of context-specific, variable ways to assess different groups. Thus, like others, we concluded that an alternative evaluation system "must be diverse enough to meet the needs of a variety of populations" (Berglund, 1989/90, p. 34). To do this, such a system should include *a set of guiding principles, a range of evaluation tools that teachers could select from, and a process of ongoing documentation*. The next pages will describe each of these.

Guiding Principles: What Characterizes Alternative Evaluation?

It's contextualized, context-specific, and variable. Literacy is seen as a socio-cultural activity rather than as a collection of discrete decontextualized skills. Assessment is therefore situated in real-life contexts, in relation to particular tasks, strategies, and purposes. It focuses on how students read and write particular kinds of texts in specific contexts and how they use what they've learned in their everyday lives (see Lytle, 1988, p. 4). The particular forms that assessment takes can vary accordingly.

It's qualitative. It involves reflective description, attempting to capture the complexity and richness of literacy learning, rather than reducing it to numbers. It looks at metacognitive and affective factors including learners' conceptions of reading and writing and how they feel about changes in their lives. The ability to use literacy to make changes and take action are valued over test results.

It's process-oriented. Rather than focus only on end-results, it is concerned with how and why learners develop.

It's ongoing and integrated with instruction. Evaluation continues throughout instruction, "serving a variety of purposes including self-assessment, placement, program monitoring, materials selection, curriculum design, teaching" (Lytle, 1988, p. 4), rather than consisting only of formal pretesting and posttesting. Teachers are an integral part of this process so that it can inform instruction. As Sauvé (1987) says, "on-going evaluation helps us to respond to current needs rather than those which have become no longer relevant"(p. 59).

It's supportive. It focuses on students' strengths rather than weaknesses—on what they *can* do not what they *can't* do. Choice is built in so that students can select texts they are able to read and tasks they want to participate in.

It's done with students not to them. Evaluation is done in students' interests rather than only to meet funders' needs. Students are "active participants, co-investigators in determining and describing their own literacy practices, strengths and strategies" (Lytle, 1988, p. 3). They may participate in choosing or designing evaluation tools and evaluating themselves, and results of assessment are shared with them. As they take on responsibility for documenting and reflecting on their own progress, the burden shifts off teachers; students become subjects rather than objects of evaluation.

It's two-way. Students participate in evaluating not only their own progress, but teacher and program dynamics as well. By evaluating each other, teachers and students take mutual responsibility; many perspectives are included in evaluation.

It's open-ended. It leaves room for and values the unexpected, instead of predetermining all acceptable outcomes. Unpredictable outcomes count and credit is given for achievements that might otherwise go unnoticed (Balliro, 1989).

A Tool Kit of Assessment Procedures

Starting up. The first group of assessment tools may be used as intake or start-up activities; they provide baseline data about what students can already do with language and literacy, how they think about it, and what they may want to do with it. We integrated many of the following into instruction rather than using them as one-on-one preinstruction placement tools.

- ♦ Informal interviews
- ♦ Language and literacy inventories
- ♦ Task-oriented oral language assessment
- ♦ Reading samples
- ♦ Writing samples
- ♦ Goal-setting activities

Along the way. The second group are ongoing in-class activities to document learning as it takes place; they are integrated into instruction on a regular basis.

- ♦ Charts/checklists
- ♦ Journals
- ♦ Group journals
- ♦ Posted journals
- ♦ Portfolios
- ♦ Class accomplishments
- ♦ Anecdotes

Looking Back. The third are activities that involve reflecting on learning, teaching, curriculum and program design at the end of a cycle; they often involve the elicitation of both teachers' and students' perceptions.

- ♦ Peer interviews
- ♦ Student-teacher conferences
- ♦ Review and repetition of earlier tasks
- ♦ Student self-evaluations
- ♦ Class evaluations
- ♦ Program evaluations

Starting Up:
Interviews and Inventories

Initial encounters with students should be genuine exchanges of information designed to set students at ease, gather information useful for curriculum development, give students a sense of the philosophy of the program, and respond to their questions and concerns. The purpose should be to find out not only about students' oral language, but also about their uses and views of language and literacy, their goals and their needs. There are a number of ways to do this: informal interviews using some of the questions that follow on pages 116-118, in-depth language inventories, and task-based activities (like responding to a problem-posing code).

Ascertain language proficiency holistically. General impressions about ability to understand questions, and answer them in minimal/elaborated ways, pronunciation, control of grammar, etc., should be noted after the interview. The interviewer should write as little as possible during the interview to set the student at ease.

Use both languages. Since one purpose of the interview is to gather substantive information, a bilingual person should be present at the interview if possible and the student's first language should be used as needed. The interview should be conducted in English as far as possible to ascertain English proficiency, changing to the first language later in order to find out about students' contexts for L1 vs. L2 usage, views, interests, and needs.

Go with the flow. For the interview to be authentically communicative, it is important that the interviewer NOT stick rigidly to a format, but rather explore and follow up on interesting issues as they arise.

Be flexible about groupings. There is no reason to stick to a one-on-one format: Small groups of students can be involved in intake discussions or problem-posing tasks or even in interviews of each other.

Don't try to cover too much. In our experience, the first encounter may touch on only a few of the areas suggested here and others may become content for early class discussions or be integrated into instruction through catalyst activities. In particular, questions about L1 and L2 usage can become student research activities; questions about schooling in the homeland can be the basis for in-class cultural comparison.

Respect privacy and give students choice. Because students may be uncomfortable with certain questions, it is important to stress that they should feel free not to answer.

Make communication two-way. The interviewer should share information about him or herself when appropriate to establish a communicative atmosphere. For example, if both the student and the interviewer have babies, they might talk about that.

Guidelines for Intake

Why: Intake should be viewed as a two-way process in which students and staff are introduced to each other. Its purpose is not just to expedite placement, but also to get a sense of what students want to do, put them at ease, and set the tone for learning. The process should reflect a participatory approach, emphasizing students' strengths by giving them plenty of opportunity to demonstrate what they *can* do (not just what they *can't* do); it must be communicative and interactive.

What: The content of placement tests and intake interviews sends a message to students about what literacy and language are. If tests stress decontextualized word lists, sound-symbol correspondences, and filling out forms, they send the message that literacy is a mechanical process, divorced from any meaningful relationship to students' lives. If, on the other hand, a range of text types, formats, and tasks are included, with interesting, semantically whole texts that are relevant to students' lives and allow for student input, a more organic, holistic view of literacy is projected. Students should be able to respond to a selection of graphics, forms, and excerpts from authentic texts (e.g., newspapers, magazines) representing real uses for literacy.

How: The format of intake also sends a message to students about how they are viewed as learners. There is an implicit power differential between students and staff that the intake process can either reinforce or challenge. It is important that the interview not be a rigidly controlled, lock-step procedure that sticks to a pre-determined format and gives students the sense that they are being judged. Rather, students must be given a sense of control and choice: They should be invited to select which items they want to respond to and how they want to respond. For example, they might be presented with a few short passages of varying content and difficulty (in either English or their first language) and asked which they would like to read. Questions should relate the readings to the students' lives, and students should be given options in responding (L1 or English, orally or in writing). Display questions (where the interviewer already knows the answer and is testing the students' knowledge) should be avoided in favor of real questions (where the student is providing new information to the interviewer). Invasive questions (like "How many people live in your house?") should be avoided since students may wonder whether this information will be used against them as it often is by authorities, thus immediately putting them on the defensive. Students should have time to ask questions about the program.

Who: Teachers should be involved in intake wherever possible. It is difficult to accurately gauge language level and appropriate placement solely through quantitative, "objective" measures; the subjective judgement necessary for accurate assessment requires the professional skill of teachers. In addition, teacher participation in intake insures that information gathered through intake can inform curriculum development. Ideally, a bilingual teacher or a team of teacher and bilingual aide team can do intake, allowing for the possibility of assessing first language literacy. If this is not possible, substantive information gathered in intake should be made available to teachers so it can be used for placement and curriculum development.

Possible Interview Questions
(adapted for ESL students from Lytle et al.'s (1986) intake conference)

These questions should be seen as guidelines to eliciting the type of information that is useful, but the information itself may be generated more successfully through in-class activities like those described in Chapter 4 of this book.

Students' background
♦ Where are you from?
♦ What was your first language?
♦ What other languages do you speak?
♦ Do you have family here?
♦ Do you have children? How many? Do you have pictures with you?
♦ How old are they? What are their names? Are they with you in the U.S.? Where do they go to school? What grades are they in? Are they in bilingual classes?

[Here the interviewer might also want to share family pictures. By this point, the interviewer should already have a sense of the student's oral English proficiency.]

Employment
♦ Did you work in your country? What kind of work did you do?
♦ Do you work here?
  [If no]: Do you want to work? What kind of work do you want to do?
  [If yes]: What kind of work do you do? Do you like it? Do you want to get another kind of job? What kind of a job?
♦ Do you do work that you're not paid for (church/community/childcare)?

Education
♦ Did you go to school in your country? For how long?
♦ Do most people in your country go to school?
♦ Did your parents go to school?
♦ What are schools like in your country?
♦ Have you gone to any other classes or schools in the U.S.?
♦ Are you teaching anyone anything now(sewing/driving/sports)?
♦ Are you teaching your children your first language? What else are you teaching them?
♦ Why did you decide to come to English class now?
♦ What kinds of things would you like to learn here?
♦ What do you hope to do with better English? How do you think learning to read and write in English will change your life?
♦ How do you think your family will feel as your English gets better?

Conceptions about literacy
♦ Do most people know how to read and write in your country?
♦ How is reading taught in your country?

Reading:
♦ Do you like to read? Why/why not?
♦ Do you read at home? What do you read? When do you read?
♦ What language or languages do you read in?
♦ What kinds of things do you read in your first language? in English?
♦ Do you read at work? What kinds of things do you read?
♦ Is it easy or hard for you to read in your first language? in English?
♦ Do you think you are a good reader? Why/why not?
♦ What is the hardest thing about learning to read in English for you?
♦ Do you know anyone who is a good reader? What makes that person a good reader? (Simpler wording: Who is a good reader? Why?)

Writing:
♦ Do you like to write? Why/why not?
♦ Do you write at home? What do you write? When do you write?
♦ What language or languages do you write in?
♦ What kinds of things do you write in each language?

♦ Do you think you are a good writer? Why/why not?
♦ What is the hardest thing about learning to write for you?
♦ Do you know someone who is a good writer? What makes that person a good writer? What does that person do?

Support systems:
♦ What do you do when you have trouble reading or writing something?
♦ Does anyone help you? Who?
♦ Do you help anyone with reading and writing? Who?
♦ Do you think it's important to read and write in both your first language and in English?
♦ Do you want to work on your first language reading and writing?
♦ Do you want your kids to learn to read and write in your first language?

Needs:
♦ What do you need English for? How do you want to use it?
♦ What do you want to do with it?

Inventory of Uses of Language and Literacy

Students can participate in open-ended research about language and literacy use in their lives, doing tasks like listing all the things they read or write in one day, or listing all the kinds of written materials in each language in their house; alternatively, questionnaires like this one can be used to guide student research, or checklists with pictures can be used to survey language use contexts.

What do you already know how to read/use in English? What do you want to learn to read?

	Already know	Want to learn
phone book		
bills		
labels on medicine bottles		
letters from friends		
newspaper		
menus		
poetry		
dictionary		
Help Wanted ads		
ads for housing		
Bible		
children's books		
movie schedules		
material for work		
directions for using things		
notes and notices from school		
stories		
other_____		

What do you already know how to write in English? What do you want to learn to write?

	Already know	Want to learn
letters		
notes to school		
diary		
poetry and stories		
homework		
forms and applications		
checks		
things for work		
other _____		

What kinds of written material are there in your house?

__children's books
__dictionaries
__magazines and comics
__newspapers
__notes from school
__letters
__TV guides
__cook books and home repair guides
__ literature: novels, poetry
__official papers
__religious books
__other_____

Reading and Writing Samples

This sequence is adapted from Lytle et al. (1986) and from formats used in our program.

Quick check. This is to get a preliminary sense of basics. It might include a simple application form (name, address, phone number, hours available for English class, etc.). The interviewer can help if the student has trouble. The interviewer can go on to check contextualized sight words (in photos of signs or labels), judging whether to continue with the writing samples based on this.

Reading selection. A range of authentic materials in the student's first language and English can be spread out on the table (e.g., newspaper, magazine, children's book, driver's manual, comic, greeting card, photonovella, poem, brochure, report card, announcement about classes). Students should be asked if they would like to read any of these or parts of them; after reading and talking about them, they should be asked which other ones (or what else) they would like to work on in class.

Writing selection. The student should be asked to choose one writing task from a range: making a quick grocery list, writing a note telling a child's teacher that the child is sick, taking a phone message, filling out a check or an application for housing, writing a postcard to a friend.

Reading whole texts. Students should be shown a packet of short texts on a variety of themes including some written by other literacy students. The interviewer may have a few packets at different levels, showing only the one deemed appropriate for that student. The texts should be semantically whole, with content related to students' lives. Students should be asked which text they want to read and asked how they want to read it (silently or aloud; together or alone) or if they want to listen only. Retelling and discussion can be either in the student's first or second language. Questions might include: Why did you pick this story? What was it about? Did it remind you of anything in your own life? Do you have any questions about it? Was there anything special you liked or didn't like about it? Teachers can note which text students chose, and how they read and responded to it (literal comprehension, inference, reacting to ideas, relating to personal experience, evaluating).

Writing whole texts. Students should be given a catalyst for writing their own stories; it might be the texts they have just read or a picture (like the learning pictures described on p. 49 or a photo they have). Again, they can be given a choice of writing in their first or second language.

Along the Way:
Ongoing
Assessment Tools

One of the most important ways to develop student participation in curriculum development and evaluation is by structuring ritualized procedures, built in on a regular daily, weekly or monthly basis, for collecting and reflecting on student work. These activities give participants immediate feedback about the effectiveness of learning and teaching, allowing adjustments to be made along the way; in addition, they provide a basis for reviewing progress at the end of the cycle.

In-class goal-setting activities. Early classes can focus on tasks designed to elicit student conceptions about language learning, student-teacher roles, and student and teacher goals for the class. Many of the activities described in Chapter 4 can be used in this way. In addition, "The English Class" (Unit I, Lesson 3 of *ESL for Action,* Auerbach and Wallerstein, 1987) includes activities to generate discussion about reasons for studying English, attitudes toward language learning, and a model for ongoing evaluation of each lesson. Andy developed a lesson (Nash, 1989) based on group responses to "It's easy to learn when____; It's hard to learn when _____." From this, a set of class resolutions emerged as the basis for evaluation.

Action evaluations. Once students have addressed a problem through individual or group action (like testifying at a funding hearing, dealing with issues of family or classroom dynamics), they can reflect on what happened with dialogue questions like: What happened? How did you feel about it? Why did it happen this way? What might you do differently next time? What new issues have arisen from this action?

Charts/checklists. Students can make charts reflecting what they can and can't do, do and don't like, want and don't want to learn. These can be done individually or as a group, daily, weekly or monthly. East End Literacy (1990) and Nunan (1988) include a range of checklist formats that can be adapted for particular groups or students. The following questions are adapted from a format suggested by Nunan (1988, p. 134):

This week I studied_____.
This week I learned_____.
This week I liked_____.
This week I didn't like:_____.
This week I used my English in these places:
This week I spoke with these people:
This week I had difficulties with_____.
I would like to know/work on_____.
My learning and practicing plans for next week are_____.

Individual student journals. Journals can be used for assessment in a number of ways. Balliro (1989) suggests building in 15 minutes at the end of each class in which the teacher and students each write journal entries. Students can reflect on their own learning, assess their progress using English, and report on accomplishments, writing about reactions to classroom experiences, interactions using English outside of class, family interactions, or anything else that is on their minds. As they develop, journals provide concrete evidence of students' progress. Teachers can evaluate them in terms of criteria like range of topics/content, elaboration of ideas (including use of details, examples, depth of analysis, emotional force, etc.), length of entries, grammatical development (specific forms like tense markers, fragments, etc.) and coherence as well as in terms of students' own perspective on their learning. Students can use them for self-evaluation by reading and responding to the finished products, noting changes and areas needing work.

The group journal. Sauvé (1987) describes a group process whereby everyone contributes reflections at the end of each class in response to questions like, "What happened today? What did we do today? What did we learn today?" This provides a sense of the differing perspectives in the group, forces the group to name what they have done, and encourages collective responsibility. It can be done as an LEA activity; journals can be collected as a class history.

The posted journal. Charo's class used an evaluation procedure that involved posting a sheet of newsprint in class with the word "Accomplishments" at the top and two columns, one called "In Class" and the other called "Out of Class". Whenever anyone had something to report that they felt good about, they wrote it on the list.

Class newsletters. Andy developed a class newsletter in which she summarized the activities of the week as a vehicle for reflecting on learning and discussing accomplishments. She included points covered in the lessons (grammar, readings, etc.), reports on class discussions, attendance, and accounts of individual students' problems or achievements. The newsletter served a number of functions, from reviewing lesson content, to becoming a reading text, to catalyzing action about class issues (like attendance), to documenting the progress of the class and becoming an evaluation tool. See "Our Class: A Weekly Literacy Ritual" in *Talking Shop* (Nash, et al., in press).

Portfolios. Student writing can be collected in individual portfolios that include everything from informal free-writing assignments to all the drafts of each piece from the beginning to the end of the cycle. These become records of development that both teachers and students evaluate periodically or at the end of the cycle. Students then see concrete representations of their own growth and they can be asked to comment on changes they note. Teachers can look for development of spelling, grammar, coherence, organization, elaboration of ideas, etc.

Anecdotes

Hemmingdinger (1988) identifies anecdotes as an important tool for legitimating the many ways that literacy changes students' lives. It defines an anecdote as "an account of someone, describing what you noticed about the student in the beginning and how the student has changed since then" (p.128). These stories describe changes that don't show up in direct paper-and-pencil assessment procedures, including affective changes in self-confidence, openness, group participation, ability to make a living, etc. In a participatory approach, they go beyond personal changes to include the ability to use literacy to address social problems: to work with others to make changes in family and community life.

Anecdotes serve two functions. First, they provide valuable feedback to the learner; because of this, they should be written with the learner in mind, using language that is accessible and content that can be shared. Second, they are a means of reporting changes to others in a systematic format. To accomplish these goals, East End Literacy suggests that anecdotes have two components, one that is descriptive and another that is analytical. The former tells the story of the incident indicating change, comparing the student before and after. The latter entails labeling or categorizing changes to provide a schema for documenting them. *This is Not a Test: A Kit for New Readers* (East End Literacy, 1990) describes in detail how to identify, keep track of, and summarize changes. It suggests a format in which the description is written on the right hand side of the page with corresponding categories of changes listed alongside them in the left margin. Categories of change can be summarized at the end of a collection of anecdotes with short phrases providing examples of each category.

The content of categories—deciding what counts as change—will vary depending on program objectives. Categories listed on the following pages are adapted and expanded from Hemmingdinger (1988); East End Literacy (1990); Isserlis and Filipek (1988); and Balliro (1989). The same factors used to analyze anecdotes can be applied in categorizing information yielded by other assessment tools (interviews, reading/writing samples, student journals, group journals, class accomplishments, etc.). The checklist format presented here is one way to capture changes graphically. The particular categories of change included here are by no means exhaustive; they should be seen as examples of possible markers of change. Categories should vary according to program and student goals. Each checklist should be specific to the learning context in which it is used!

Progress Checklist			
Name _____ Date _____			
	Before cycle	**During cycle**	**End of cycle**
Personal, affective changes:			
♦ feeling safe, feeling at ease			
♦ willing to take risks			
♦ longer attention span			
♦ ability to identify personal learning goals			
♦ ability to address personal problems			
♦ other _____			
Social changes in the classroom/among peers:			
♦ increased self-direction of learning			
♦ increased participation			
♦ self-monitoring of participation			
♦ ability to help and support peers			
♦ ability to express opinion or disagree			
♦ ability to take on new roles (leadership)			
♦ ability to reflect on classroom dynamics			
♦ other _____			
Social changes outside the classroom:			
♦ participation in community activities, organizations			
♦ increased responsibility			
♦ social networking			
♦ using community resources			
♦ assisting, supporting peers			
♦ other _____			
Changes in relation to children's schooling:			
♦ more support at home			
♦ more contact with school			
♦ advocacy on children's behalf			
♦ participation in parent groups			
♦ other _____			
Changes in writing			
♦ mechanics (letter formation, spelling, etc.)			
♦ length of written pieces			
♦ ability to generate ideas			
♦ ability to draft and revise			
♦ elaboration of ideas			
♦ organization			
♦ ability to write about personal experience			
♦ ability to write analytically			
♦ other _____			

	Before cycle	During cycle	End of cycle
Changes in reading ♦ predicting ♦ using prior knowledge ♦ skimming, previewing ♦ using context ♦ guessing ♦ sound/letter/word identification ♦ awareness of strategies ♦ ability to relate reading to personal experience ♦ critical reading ♦ other _____ .			
Changes in oral language use ♦ comprehension ♦ ability to ask for clarification ♦ clarity of pronunciation ♦ immediacy of response ♦ length of utterances ♦ taking the initiative ♦ taking risks ♦ ability to express opinions ♦ ability to question/challenge ♦ other _____			
Metacognitive changes ♦ awareness of progress/goals ♦ awareness of reading/writing processes ♦ ability to monitor and choose strategies ♦ ability to ask for assistance ♦ ability to make choices about language use ♦ other _____			

Changes in uses of literacy
♦ functional uses in specific contexts
  • consumer choice
  • employment
  • housing
  • banking/money
  • health care
♦ using literacy for personal expression
♦ using literacy in family interactions
♦ using literacy for learning
♦ using literacy for advocacy
♦ increased independence in literacy use
♦ using literacy to understand social context
♦ using literacy to question and challenge
♦ other _____			

Looking Back:
End of Cycle
Evaluations

The following activities for the end of the cycle invite students and teachers to reflect on what they have and haven't accomplished; again students should have the option of doing these in either English or their first language.

Peer interviews. Students can interview each other using questions they have generated collectively. These may be framed in terms of initial goals or more general questions like "What are the most important things you learned in this class? What can you do now that you couldn't do before? What changes have you made since you began this class? What did you like most about this class? What should be changed about the class?" Students can report each other's answers to the whole group and compare impressions.

Student-teacher conferences. Students and teachers can use the same questions they started with at intake, comparing before and after responses.

Review and repetition of earlier tasks. Students can review their portfolios, journals, and coursework to see changes. They can repeat reading and writing sample tasks and compare results; this can be done individually, with peers, or with the teacher.

Student self-evaluations. Students can use chart, checklist or narrative writing formats to evaluate their own learning. If they used checklists to identify goals, interests, and needs earlier, they can come back to these and determine whether their goals have been met and what they still need to work on. See Nunan (1988, pp.131-134).

Class evaluations. Students can be invited to provide feedback about the class either during or at the end of a cycle. Because students are often reluctant to express negative feelings or criticism, questions should be impersonal; students can be asked to write anonymous evaluations or work in groups so that no individual's ideas are identified. In addition, it helps to have specific questions about what participants disliked or would change. For a beginning class, Ann used questions like "How do you usually feel in class? Is the class too easy or difficult for you? What could improve the class?" At a higher level, she asked, "What kind of atmosphere did you expect to find in classes before you came? What did you find that you didn't expect to find? What didn't you find that you expected to find? In what situations did you use what you learned in the class? What were the games you learned the most from?"

Program evaluation. Students from various classes can come together to discuss programmatic issues like class structure, content, use of the native language, childcare, scheduling, class size, groupings, and funding concerns. Ann Cason details the processes and benefits of this kind of evaluation in *Talking Shop* ("All-Program Evaluations").

Teacher Research: Ongoing Documentation Procedures

Finally, teachers can document their own curriculum development processes through the following:

♦ Retroactive lesson plans
♦ Teachers' journals
♦ Tape recordings
♦ Monthly reports
♦ Minutes of meetings

The cornerstone of qualitative evaluation is documenting what is happening in the classroom as it happens. As Johnston (1989, p. 509) says,

> Central to this approach is the teacher's ability to know the students, and to notice and record their development in a variety of areas...the ability to set the conditions for and to notice patterns of activity and changes in those patterns is at the heart of the teacher's evaluative skill.

This kind of evaluation provides the context within which to understand students' progress, the basis for curriculum decision-making, and a record of changes that can become data for further analysis. Thus, teachers become researchers of their own classrooms.

Both the process and the product of documenting curriculum development serve important functions. Since documentation is done in an open-ended, descriptive way—collecting and recording data without predetermining what to look for (as in ethnographic research)—the process itself becomes a vehicle for listening to and valuing the unexpected. It enables the teacher to stand back from the immediate moment and reflect on it, which, in turn, may lead to new insights about patterns and issues. Just by writing or talking about what is happening in their classes, teachers gain new understandings of why it is happening and what to do next.

Very often, however, insights about what is happening don't come until much later. It may not be clear how to use information as it is being gathered. Thus, the ongoing accounts can serve a retroactive function, becoming "data" for future reflection; they provide invaluable information as recorded histories of class cycles, student progress, and teacher thinking. Teachers in our project, for example, collected teaching materials, student writings, notes, and journal-like descriptions of particular teaching cycles. While they were in the middle of the cycles, they had one perspective on them, but when they wrote about them later, their perspectives changed: "Putting our experiences down on paper, we have been forced to reflect on them as we may not have previously done. In this way, we've learned not only from each others' writings but from our own as well" (Nash et al., in press). Likewise, it was the cumulative, detailed documentation of day to day activities, discussions, and student work that provided the data for the analysis which has emerged in writing this curriculum guide. There are many forms of documentation ranging from very structured and schematic to open-ended and flexible. Some that we have used are described on the next pages.

Retroactive lesson plan forms. A uniform format for keeping track of activities and student reactions to them can be used on a daily or weekly basis. We started with a documentation chart with columns for noting where themes came from (catalysts), how they were developed (tools/activities), how language work was incorporated, what new issues emerged, and teacher's reflections. Although teachers in our project felt it was artificial and inhibited rich description, others might find it useful, particularly in moving from a traditional to a participatory approach.

Teachers' journals. Teachers in our project felt that journals were a more organic way of documenting day to day classroom interactions. They are more open-ended and personal. Journal entries, taken together, become a kind of history of the development of the curriculum as well as a record of particular events. While they at first seem time-consuming, the payoff is worthwhile, as Lucille Fandel (one of my graduate students at the time) writes here (personal communication, May, 1990):

> Taking time to keep a journal after every class made a qualitative difference in my teaching, helped that lessons flow better. Before, I'd do a lesson plan based on how much we'd "covered" of my previous plan. With my journaling I've found that I remember significant things that happen (often very fast, in a fleeting way) in class. This way I can pick up on them. They are the "stuff" of people's lives/of our personal interactions/of their evaluations of the class or of their own progress. Journaling has helped me see more clearly where the "flow" is going.

Family literacy teachers kept journals in which they described activities, student reactions, issues, or concerns that arose for them, their own reactions or reflections about the interactions, and ideas for future lessons.

Tape recording. Taping classroom interactions can provide raw data for future analysis. Madeline used tape recording for the purpose of monitoring small group discussions to get a sense of how one group was doing while she was working with another. Listening to the tapes revealed both interesting student issues and areas for language work. She shared the tapes with the whole class in the form of transcriptions. Thus, students could themselves reflect on the interactions, exploring both the content and linguistic aspects together. In this way, the documentation fed into instruction and students were involved in the analysis.

We also used tapes to compare reactions to materials and activities. When teachers used the same code to generate dialogue about homework, Andy taped each class on the day it was used and transcribed the tapes as a basis for teachers to analyze and compare responses. Since each group reacted differently depending on how the lesson was introduced and who the students were, the transcription enabled teachers to see concretely how the context shaped dialogue.

Monthly reports. Summaries of the month's activities provide an overview of activities, accomplishments, and issues for groups. The process of writing these reports can be a framework for reflection, a time for teachers to think about what they've done and where they're going. The reports can also provide a place to communicate problems, needs, and concerns to program administration. Depending on the point in program development, these might address questions about recruitment, intake, students, classroom activities, critical incidents or anecdotes, new insights, ideas, or issues (what you've learned about your own teaching, reflections, goals, challenges). It is also helpful to include examples of materials, student work, journal entries, and retroactive lesson plans.

Minutes of meetings. There are several limitations to these forms of documentation done by individual teachers. First, they take more time than many teachers have. Second, while each may reflect what's happening in particular classes, separately they may be fragmented and fall short of reflecting the broader picture for a project. Third, because by nature they are the result of an individual process, they preclude the kind of insight that comes from collective analysis. Thus, the dialogue that takes place in teacher meetings and the recording of that dialogue through minutes are central to the curriculum development and evaluation process. The meetings provide a framework for the development of a "community of knowledgeable peers" (Balliro, 1989) and a context for the program-based practitioner research called for by Lytle (1988). The minutes provide a detailed, sequential documentation of what transpires in this process; they become the thread that ties together individual accounts.

Putting it All Together: A Context-Specific Approach to Evaluation

Although the system of evaluation proposed here isn't neatly packaged into a ready-made sequence, we hope it will be useful as programs construct their own evaluation schemes. Specifically, we hope that its rationale and principles can help to challenge demands for standardized testing and to justify qualitative approaches to evaluation, that the "toolkit" can be a resource as programs select and adapt tools for their own contexts, and that the documentation processes will help teachers gather information that is useful for their own curriculum development as well as for reporting to others (administrators and funders). Most importantly, however, the results of this kind of evaluation will help to develop the field of adult education. As more and more practitioners document, analyze, and share what they're doing, our collective understanding of what does and doesn't work will grow so that research that comes from inside the classroom will become the basis for constructing and extending our knowledge about adult learning.

Conclusion: Looking Back, Looking Ahead

From the body of data gathered following the processes outlined in Chapter 8, we were able to make a number of generalizations about adult ESL teaching and learning that have implications for the field as a whole. Specifically, findings from our work suggest the following:

When the content of ESL literacy instruction is related to students' lives, both the quantity and quality of their reading and writing increase significantly. In some cases, student writing doubled when the focus shifted from decontextualized skills and grammar work to social-contextual issues (daycare, immigration, etc.). Even the lowest level students were capable of sophisticated conceptual analysis when literacy work centered on meaning rather than form. Thus, a bottom-up view of literacy acquisition that limits beginning students to decoding, decontextualized skills and functional language use may impede language and literacy development.

If reading, writing, speaking, and grammar are integrated, rather than being separated as isolated skills, students are able to perform conceptually and linguistically more sophisticated tasks. When instruction was organized around content rather than skills, students were able to develop ideas through a variety of modes (conversation, reading, and writing), resulting in richer, more meaningful language use. When grammar was taught in isolation, students often had difficulty internalizing rules and transferring them to other contexts. Thus, when grammar instruction is embedded in content-based, meaning-making tasks, it seems to be easier for students to monitor, internalize, and transfer appropriate usage.

Interest and engagement are greater when students are involved in determining the content of the curriculum. Our students were often more responsive to themes that they had identified than to those introduced by the teacher; in some cases, they responded better to texts they had written than to texts with similar content written by someone else. Even for teacher-identified issues, students were more engaged if they had a choice about pursuing them.

Students are interested in a broad range of issues and literacy uses beyond functional or survival topics. The diversity of topics that emerged in our project indicates that adult ESL students want more than a narrow life skills focus. In particular, it shows that bilingual parents may want to address a variety of concerns in addition to those related directly to their children's schooling or literacy acquisition.

The quality of students' reading and writing increases when they are presented as social, collaborative processes rather than individual ones. When students worked together, they were often able to read and write longer, more conceptually complex and linguistically sophisticated pieces. Through the group process, they were able to use literacy to make changes outside the classroom. This finding suggests that peer learning serves an important function in literacy acquisition and raises questions about programs based solely on one-to-one tutoring.

Attendance, retention, and students' responsibility for their own learning increase when they are involved in decision-making. When teachers brought issues of classroom dynamics, curriculum choices, and evaluation to students (as content for literacy work), there were significant changes in their attitudes and participation. They were able to monitor and change personal and group learning patterns.

Use of the first language can be a powerful tool for second language, literacy, and conceptual development. In contrast to the prevalent view that ESL acquisition is facilitated by using English only, our work suggests that selective use of the second language can be beneficial. By providing first language literacy instruction, we were able to reach a population of students who had previously been excluded. Further, by giving ESL students choices about language use, both the conceptual level of their literacy work and the quality of what they produced in English were enhanced. Thus, for many students, using the first language as a bridge facilitates the acquisition of English. Finally, when students are involved in reflecting on and making language choices, they become monitors of their own language use.

What Made It Possible?

Looking back at our own experience, we identified three key factors that made it possible for students to achieve as much as they did and for teachers to make the innovations and reach the conclusions presented in this book.

First was *the atmosphere of inquiry and experimentation* that permeated the project. Rather than starting with givens, we approached our work openly, constantly trying new things and analyzing what did or didn't work. No one defined from the outside what teachers should be doing; instead teachers had the freedom to investigate content, methods, tools, and activities with students.

Second was *the structure for teacher-sharing*. Instituting a regular, legitimated time and place for raising concerns, getting feedback, and reflecting collectively on what was happening in classrooms served a number of functions. As a form of staff development, it allowed for cross-fertilization between classes, with teachers learning from each other, taking ideas from one context and applying them in another. Teachers became their own best resources in generating curriculum material. Teacher-sharing also provided a support system for teachers. By sharing doubts, problems and successes, they were able to energize each other and combat the isolation that teachers so often feel. Most importantly from a research perspective, teacher-sharing provided a way to generalize from individual experience; as teachers examined and compared findings from one context to another, they gained a broader perspective on their own practice, identified patterns. and moved toward generalizations.

Third was *the fact that we applied the same participatory principles to our work as a group* that we used in our teaching. Just as teacher-student roles get redefined in a participatory classroom, we gradually moved toward equalizing our roles within the project staff. We tried to make decisions together, identify topics for training together, and construct our collective knowledge together. We shifted toward sharing responsibility for dissemination and conference presentations. Several of our publications were the result of attempts at participatory production. While this process was uneven and we may not ever have reached our goal of becoming fully participatory, the fact that we had this goal enabled participants to voice their concerns and see struggles for an equalization of roles as legitimate. It gave us a standard against which to measure our practice as a group and ensured that there was a forum for talking about issues of participation and decision-making.

Implications for the Future: Making the Transition to a Participatory Approach

While the approach we have outlined in this book is a powerful one, it clearly requires a great deal of time and energy. For teachers, the biggest concern is often that it sounds like too much work! In reading this guide, you may very well feel overwhelmed and wonder where to start or how to deal with administrators who don't share the perspectives presented here. These are realistic concerns that shouldn't be minimized; the following suggestions may help in addressing them.

First, rather than throwing out everything you're comfortable with and seeing this approach as a complete change from past practice, it may make more sense to begin by building bridges between what you're already doing and what's new to you. Teachers, like students, need to mix the old with the new. Chapter 1 presented an example of a lesson in which students were asked to respond to a school flyer listing ways that they should help their children with homework. In that lesson, Loren asked the students to look at the flyer critically, addressing questions like:

♦ Which of these things do you already do?
♦ Which of these things would you like to do?
♦ Which do you think are ridiculous, unrealistic or impossible?
♦ What do you already do that's not listed here?

You might want to ask the same questions about this book, starting by examining your existing practice. Ask yourself what you are already doing that works well (identifying what seems to get the most/least student response), and figure out why. Further, you can find commonalities between the two approaches: Examine what you are already doing that is similar to something you read about in this guide and try to build on that. Then you can begin experimenting with new ideas on a limited basis. You might do nothing but record issues that you identify through conscious listening, building a core of topics for future exploration; or you might experiment with finding themes using the methods described in Chapter 4. Or you might choose one theme that is obviously "hot" and develop a curriculum unit around it (including a code or other tools described in Chapter 5). The point is to start small, making the transition to a new approach gradually. In this process, it may be helpful to keep a journal in which you record issues as they come up, write observations, and evaluate the new things you try.

Second, you can begin establishing a support network. Since the teacher's role is one of posing rather than solving problems, you don't have to do everything alone: Your students and your colleagues are partners in the process. This means working with students to figure out themes, activities, and directions. Once you share this process with them and stop feeling that you have to be the source of all knowledge and direction, the burden is lightened. Teachers often say that when they realize that they don't have to be the authority in the classroom who solves every problem and has answers to every question, they feel relieved. Your co-workers are an invaluable resource; teachers can exchange ideas for catalysts, materials, exercises, and ways of dealing with students' issues or class dynamics.

Third, it is helpful to know that the process of finding themes and using tools becomes routine in a relatively short time. Issues begin to spring up everywhere once you're tuned in to them. As you develop a core collection of authentic texts and sources of photographs like those listed in Additional Resources, it's not hard to find relevant materials. But most importantly, once you become familiar with a few basic processes (linking reading to students' experiences, developing codes, guiding dialogue, writing collaboratively, going through the stages of the writing process, developing class newsletters, etc.), responding to issues as they arise becomes second nature. The key is having the conceptual framework: the understanding that content must come from and go back to students' lives.

Finally, once this process begins, it starts to have its own payoff. It's no longer necessary to ignore the diversions, or feel guilty for digressing into unplanned discussions. The quality and content of student responses are often more rich and varied than they are in a grammar or competency-driven curriculum. And most of all, it's fun! The level of sharing and communication becomes a reward in itself.

It is also certainly true that teachers need the support and cooperation of funders and program administrators to implement a participatory approach. The effectiveness of this approach will be curtailed if teachers constantly feel constrained by external demands based on conflicting assumptions. Funders and program administrators play a critical role in creating the conditions necessary for an effective program. It is important for them to give teachers the time and flexibility to develop curricula specific to the needs of their students. Specific structural guidelines for doing this are presented in the Practitioners' Bill of Rights (p. 37). Central among these is providing paid time for teacher sharing, planning, and staff development; further, evaluation procedures that reflect language and literacy usage both inside and outside the classroom must be developed and adopted. In addition, it is critical to treat teachers as knowledgeable professionals, giving them both the autonomy and the support needed to develop appropriate curricula.

Finally, it is important for funders, administrators, and practitioners to work together to educate legislators about adult literacy and to advocate for the kind of programming described here. As long as literacy is seen narrowly in terms of employment-related outcomes, and legislation focuses on job-preparedness, certain segments of the student population will be excluded and others may be relegated to dead-end entry-level jobs.

Digging With a Teaspoon... or Putting It All in Perspective

At one point, Andy made the comment that sometimes it feels like we're digging with a teaspoon in the desert. Change happens slowly and our efforts may seem small in relation to the enormity of the issues facing students. Further, administrators want to see fast results and often blame the teachers or the approach if changes aren't immediate or visible enough. There seems to be an expectation that if only we, as adult educators, find the right approach or are effective enough inside the classroom, students will make dramatic leaps in proficiency with consequences for all the other social and economic problems they face.

It is important for both teachers and administrators to remember that language, literacy, and adult education are pieces of a bigger picture. We started this book with the analysis that family literacy is shaped by many factors: by whether families have an adequate place to live, adequate jobs, and health care. For many adult ESL students, the pressures of immigration, poor housing conditions, health problems, employment concerns (unemployment, low wages, having to work several jobs, substandard working conditions, etc.) are the central realities of daily life. It is an illusion to think that literacy is a magic bullet that will solve these problems. No matter how well classes are taught, unless the basic inequities in the socioeconomic conditions of students' lives outside the classroom are also addressed, what happens inside the classroom will be of minor significance. It is unrealistic to expect that by addressing one piece of this picture, the others will be resolved. Blaming ineffective educational methods for problems whose source lies elsewhere becomes a kind of scapegoating. By the same token, it is unrealistic to think that literacy work, no matter how participatory, will in itself lead to social transformation. Although Freire-inspired literacy campaigns have often been accompanied by deep-seated social changes, their power may have come from the fact that these changes were already taking place.

Clearly, this is not to say that what happens in the classroom doesn't matter. The approach to literacy can either contribute to students' ability to take on some of the other social-contextual issues or reinforce a sense of futility. The rationale for the approach proposed in this book is that literacy instruction *can* make a difference if its focus is on linking curriculum content to the struggle for change in the socioeconomic conditions of students' lives. But it's important to keep in mind that literacy work is only one front in a larger struggle, and, by itself, it isn't a solution. It will be most effective when it is connected to this larger context rather than seen as a self-contained endeavor, or goal in itself.

Thus, it makes sense to think of circles of change moving from classroom practice to program structure to the broader socioeconomic context. Hopefully this book will be a concrete tool in each of these circles of change. In terms of the first circle, we hope that the guide provides not just a "how to," but a framework for looking critically at your own practice, as well as adapting and adding to what is presented here. In terms of the second circle, the guide may serve as a source of support in the struggle to create changes in structural aspects of adult literacy work. Specifically, we hope the sections on rationale, program structure, curriculum development processes, evaluation, and findings will be used in advocating for changes with legislators, funders, administrators, and program designers.

Third, we hope that this guide will be a resource for linking literacy programs to other structures and organizations addressing the underlying socioeconomic issues facing students: organizations dealing with workplace, housing, or health care concerns as well as with family literacy. It may be useful in developing context-specific curricula that emerge from and are integrated with the ongoing activities of these groups. Making meaning inside the classroom will extend to making change outside the classroom as adult ESL/literacy work becomes one arena among many, connected to a broader process of transforming the conditions in students' lives.

A final word from students:

If you speak English good, read English good, and write English good, you can work for more money.

We want to read English, write English and speak English. 3 hours of school is not enough. We want more hours. We want books, too. We want the government to help us.

References

Arnold, R., Barndt, D., & Burke, B. (1985). *A new weave: Popular education in Canada and Central America.* Toronto: Canadian University Services Overseas and OISE Press.

Auerbach, E. (1986). Competency-based ESL: One step forward or two steps back? *TESOL Quarterly, 20,* 411-429.

Auerbach, E. (Ed.). (1989a). Nontraditional materials for adult ESL. *TESOL Quarterly, 23,* 321-335.

Auerbach, E. (1989b). Toward a social-contextual approach to family literacy. *Harvard Educational Review, 59,* 165-181.

Auerbach, E., & McGrail, L. (1991). Rosa's challenge: Connecting classroom and community contexts. In S. Benesch (Ed.), *ESL in America: Myths and possibilities* (pp. 96-111). Portsmouth, NH: Boynton/Cook.

Auerbach, E., & Wallerstein, N. (1987). *ESL for action: Problem-posing at work. Teachers' guide.* Reading, MA: Addison-Wesley.

Balliro, L. (1989, March). *Reassessing assessment in adult ESL/literacy.* Paper presented at the annual conference of Teachers of English to Speakers of Other Languages, San Antonio, TX. (ERIC Document Reproduction Service No. ED 339 253)

Barndt, D. (n.d.). *Just getting there: Creating visual tools for collective analysis.* Toronto: Participatory Research Group.

Barndt, D. (1986). *English at work: A tool kit for teachers.* North York, Ontario: CORE Foundation. (OP. See Barndt, Belfiore, & Hanscombe, 1991, for revised edition.)

Barndt, D. (1987). *Themes and tools for ESL: How to choose them and use them.* Toronto: Ministry of Citizenship, Province of Ontario.

Barndt, D., Belfiore, M.E., & Hanscombe, J. (1991). *English at work: A tool kit for teachers* (rev. ed.). Syracuse, NY: New Readers Press.

Berglund, R.L. (1989/90, Winter). Convention sessions address whole language evaluation. *Reading Today,* p. 34.

Candlin, C. (1984). Syllabus design as a critical process. In C.J. Brumfit (Ed.), *General English syllabus design* (pp. 29-46). Oxford: Pergamon Press.

Carrell, P., Devine, J., & Eskey, D. (1988). *Interactive approaches to second language reading.* Cambridge: Cambridge University Press.

Carver, T., & Fotinos, S. (1985). *A conversation book: English in everyday life, Book 2.* Englewood Cliffs, NJ: Prentice-Hall.

Chall, J.S., & Snow, C. (1982). *Families and literacy: The contributions of out of school experiences to children's acquisition of literacy* [The Harvard Families and Literacy Project final report]. Washington, DC: National Institute of Education.

Delgado-Gaitan, C. (1987). Mexican adult literacy: New directions for immigrants. In S.R. Goldman & K. Trueba (Eds.), *Becoming literate in English as a second language* (pp. 9-32). Norwood, NJ: Ablex.

Dugan, S., Skinner, J., & Tirone, P. (1987). *Adult ESL students vs. the TABE: Divorce recommended.* Unpublished manuscript.

East End Literacy. (1990). *This is not a test: A kit for new readers.* Toronto: East End Literacy Press. (Distributed by Dominie Press)

Freire, P. (1970). *Pedagogy of the oppressed.* New York: Seabury Press.

Freire, P. (1981). *Education for critical consciousness.* New York: Continuum.

Freire, P., & Macedo, D. (1987). *Literacy: Reading the word and the world.* South Hadley, MA: Bergin-Garvey.

Gee, J. (1986). Orality and literacy: From *The Savage Mind* to *Ways with Words. TESOL Quarterly, 20,* 719-746.

Heath, S.B. (1983). *Ways with words.* Cambridge: Cambridge University Press.

Heath, S.B., & Branscombe, A. (1985). "Intelligent writing" in an audience community: Teachers, students, and researcher. In S.W. Freedman (Ed.), *The acquisition of written language: Response and revision* (pp. 3-32). Norwood, NJ: Ablex.

Hemmingdinger, A. (1988). *The kit: Self evaluation exercises for students and literacy workers.* Toronto: East End Literacy Press. (OP. See East End Literacy, 1990, for revised edition.)

Hope, A., & Timmel, S. (1984). *Training for transformation.* Giveru, Zimbabwe: Mambo Press.

Hughes, L. (1974). *Selected poems.* New York: Vintage.

International Reading Association. (1988). *Resolution on reading assessment.* Newark, DE: Author.

Isserlis, J., & Filipek, F. (1988). *Learner evaluation worksheet.* Handout distributed at a workshop presented at the Providence Literacy Center, Providence, RI.

Johnston, P. (1989). Constructive evaluation and the improvement of teaching and learning. *Teachers College Record, 90,* 509-528.

Kasser, C., & Silverman, A. (1986). *Stories we brought with us: Beginning readings for ESL.* Englewood Cliffs, NJ: Prentice-Hall.

Knowles, M. (1984). *Andragogy in action.* San Francisco: Jossey-Bass.

Long, L., & Podnecky, J.S. (1988). *In print: Beginning literacy through cultural awareness.* Reading, MA: Addison-Wesley.

Lytle, S.L. (1988). From the inside out: Reinventing assessment. *Focus on Basics, 2*(1), 1-4.

Lytle, S.L., Marmor, T.W., & Penner, F.H. (1986, April). *Literacy theory in practice: Assessing reading and writing of low-literate adults.* Paper presented at the annual meeting of the American Educational Research Association, San Francisco.

Martin, R. (1989). *Literacy from the inside out.* Watertown, MA: Author.

Mason, J. (1979a). *The family of children.* New York: The Ridge Press.

Mason, J. (1979b). *The family of women.* New York: The Ridge Press.

Molinsky, S., & Bliss, B. (1983). *Line by line.* Englewood Cliffs, NJ: Prentice Hall Regents.

Molinsky, S., & Bliss, B. (1988). *Side by side.* Englewood Cliffs, NJ: Prentice Hall Regents.

Nash, A. (1989). An experiment in evaluation. *All Write News, 6*(3), 1-4.

Nash, A., Cason, A., Gomez-Sanford, R., McGrail, L., & Rhum, M. (in press). *Talking shop: A sourcebook for participatory curriculum development.* McHenry, IL: Delta Systems and Center for Applied Linguistics.

Nunan, D. (1988). *The learner-centered curriculum.* Cambridge: Cambridge University Press.

Paul, M. (Ed.). (1986). *Preventive mental health in the ESL classroom: A handbook for teachers.* New York: American Council for Nationalities Service. (Attn: PP/MH, 95 Madison Ave., New York, NY 10016)

Sauvé, V. (1987). *From one educator to another: A window on participatory education.* Edmonton, Alberta: Grant MacEwan Community College.

South West African People's Organization (SWAPO). (1986). *Literacy promoter's handbook.* Luanda: Author. (Distributed by Namibia Refugee Project, 22 Coleman Fields, London N1 7AF, England)

Steichen, E. (1955). *The family of man.* New York: The Museum of Modern Art.

Street, B.V. (1984). *Literacy in theory and practice.* Cambridge: Cambridge University Press.

Strohmeyer, B., & McGrail, L. (1988). *On FOCUS: Photographs and writings by students.* Boston: El Centro del Cardenal.

Taylor, D. (1983). *Family literacy: Young children learning to read and write.* Portsmouth, NH: Heinemann.

Taylor, D. (1989). *Toward a unified theory of literacy learning and instructional practices.* Unpublished manuscript.

Taylor, D., & Dorsey-Gaines, C. (1988). *Growing up literate: Learning from inner-city families.* Portsmouth, NH: Heinemann.

Wallerstein, N. (1983). *Language and culture in conflict: Problem-posing in the ESL classroom.* Reading, MA: Addison-Wesley.

Wallerstein, N. (1991). *Freirean praxis in health education.* Unpublished manuscript.

Additional Resources

Family Literacy

Diaz, S., Moll, L., & Mehan, H. (1986). Socio-cultural resources in instruction: A context-specific approach. In California State Department of Education and California State University, *Beyond language: Social and cultural factors in schooling language minority children.* Los Angeles: Authors.

Nash, A. (1987). *English family literacy: An annotated bibliography.* Boston: University of Massachusetts, English Family Literacy Project.

Participatory Curriculum Development: Theory and Overview

Association for Community Based Education. *Literacy for empowerment: A resource handbook for community based education.* (Available from ACBE, 1806 Vernon St. NW, Washington, DC 20009)

Auerbach, E., & Burgess, D. (1985). The hidden curriculum of survival ESL. *TESOL Quarterly, 19,* 475-495.

Bell, J., & Burnaby, B. (1984). *A handbook for ESL literacy.* Toronto: OISE Press.

Fingeret, A. (1984). *Adult literacy education: Current and future directions.* Columbus, OH: ERIC Clearinghouse on Adult, Career and Vocational Education. (Ohio State University, 1900 Kenny Rd., Columbus, OH 43210-1090)

Fingeret A., & Jurmo, P. (1989). *Participatory literacy education.* San Francisco: Jossey-Bass.

Freire, P. (1985). *The politics of education: Culture, power and liberation.* South Hadley, MA: Bergin-Garvey.

Gillespie, M. (1990). *Many literacies: Modules for training adult beginning readers and tutors.* Amherst, MA: University of Massachusetts, Center for International Education. (285 Hills House, Amherst, MA 01003)

Luttrell, W. (1982). *Building multi-cultural awareness: A teaching approach for learner-centered education.* Philadelphia: Lutheran Settlement House Women's Program.

Marshall, J. (1985). *Training for empowerment: A kit of materials for popular literacy workers based on an exchange among educators from Mozambique, Nicaragua, and Brazil.* Toronto: International Council for Adult Education. (720 Bathurst St., Suite 500, Toronto, Canada M5S 2R4)

Shor, I. (1987). *Freire for the classroom.* Portsmouth, NH: Boynton/Cook, Heinemann.

Srinivasan, L. (1977). *Perspectives on non-formal adult education.* Boston: World Education.

Young, E., & Padilla, M. (1990). Mujeres unidas en acción: A popular education process. *Harvard Educational Review, 60,* 1-18.

Participatory Curriculum Development: Tools

Alojado, C. (1987). Learning to write: A demonstration project. *Passage, 3*(2), 27-31.

Amoroso, H.C. (1985). Organic primers for basic literacy instruction. *Journal of Reading, 28,* 398-401.

Barndt, D., Cristall, F., & Marino, D. (1982). *Getting there: Producing photo-stories with immigrant women.* Toronto: Between the Lines.

Boal, A. (1985). *Theatre of the oppressed.* New York: Theater Communications Group.

Cain, B.J., & Comings, J.P. (1977). *The participatory process: Producing photo-literature.* Amherst, MA: University of Massachusetts, Center for International Education. (285 Hills House, Amherst, MA 01003)

Cohen, C. (1983). Building multicultural and intergenerational networks through oral history. *Frontiers, 7,* 1-5.

Cohen, C. (1987). *Designing an oral history project: A workbook for teachers and community workers.* Cambridge: The Oral History Center.

Ellowitch, A. (1983). *A curriculum in employment: Women and the world of work.* Philadelphia: Lutheran Settlement House Women's Program.

Faigin, S. (1985). *Basic ESL literacy from a Freirean perspective: A curriculum unit for farmworker education.* Unpublished manuscript. (ERIC Document Reproduction Service No. ED 274 196)

Hawkins, C. (1984). *Teaching reading through oral histories.* Philadelphia: Lutheran Settlement House Women's Program.

Kazemek, F.E. (1985). Stories of our lives: Interviews and oral histories for language development. *Journal of Reading, 29,* 211-218.

Mantle, A. (1982). *ESL and community groups create learning materials: Four case studies.* Toronto: Participatory Research Group.

Nettle, M.E. (1982). The process and the product: Two English classes develop materials. *TESL Talk, 13*(4), 121-134.

Peyton, J.K., & Staton, J. (Eds.). (1991). *Writing our lives: Reflections on dialogue journal writing with adults learning English.* Englewood Cliffs, NJ: Prentice Hall Regents and The Center for Applied Linguisitics.

Pratt, S. (Ed.). (1982). English in the workplace. *TESL Talk, 13* (4), 58-65.

Price, P,. & Montgomery, S. (n.d.). *English as a second language: Sb/1b resource manual.* Edmonton: Alberta Vocational College. (10215 108 St., Edmonton, Alberta, Canada T5J 1L6)

Randall, M. (1985). *Testimonios: A guide to oral history.* Toronto: Participatory Research Group.

Rigg, P. (1987). Using the language experience approach with ESL adults. *TESL Talk, 20*(1), 188-200.

Wallace, C. (1988). *Learning to read in a multi-cultural society: The social context of second language literacy.* New York: Prentice Hall International.

Classroom Resources:
ESL Texts

(See Nash, Cason, Gomez-Sanford, McGrail, & Rhum, in press, for an expanded list of classroom resources.)

Auerbach, E., & Wallerstein, N. (1987). *ESL for action: Problem-posing at work.* Reading, MA: Addison-Wesley.

Bodman, J.W., & McKay, J.B. (1987). *Spaghetti again.* New York: Collier McMillan.

Carver, T., & Fotinos, S. (1977). *A conversation book: English in everyday life. Books 1 & 2.* Englewood Cliffs, NJ: Prentice-Hall.

Ellowitch, A. (1986). *Tell me about it: Reading and language activities around multi-cultural issues based on an oral history approach.* Philadelphia: LaSalle University. (Available from Urban Studies and Community Services Center, La Salle University, 5501 Wister St., Philadelphia, PA 19144)

Kuntz, L. (1982). *The new arrival. Books 1 & 2.* Hayward, CA: Alemany Press.

Lutheran Settlement House Women's Program. (1988). *Remembering, Books 1 & 2.* Syracuse, NY: New Readers Press.

McKay, S., & Petitt, D. (1984). *At the door: Selected literature for ESL students.* Englewood Cliffs, NJ: Prentice-Hall.

Reed, F. (1987). *Feelings, thoughts and dreams: Writing and conversation starters for ESL literacy.* Syracuse, NY: New Readers Press.

Classroom Resources:
Non-Traditional/
Authentic Materials

Alvarado, E. (1987). *Don't be afraid, gringo: A Honduran woman speaks from the heart.* San Francisco: The Institute for Food and Development Policy. (145 9th St., San Francisco, CA 94103)

Cisneros, S. (1991). *The house on Mango Street.* New York: Random House.

Higgins, J., & Ross, J. (1986). *Southeast Asians: A new beginning in Lowell.* Lowell, MA: Mill Town Graphics. (Available from Cambodian Mutual Assistance Association of Lowell, 125 Perry St., Lowell, MA 01852)

Kingston, M.H. (1977). *China men.* New York: Ballantine.

Kingston, M.H. (1978). *The woman warrior.* New York: Vintage.

Morales, A., & Morales, R. (1986). *Getting home alive.* Ithaca, NY: Firebrand Books.

Oral History Center. (1987). *The mango tree: Stories told and retold by children in the Cambridge public schools.* Cambridge, MA: Author.

Patai, D. (1988). *Brazilian women speak.* New Brunswick, NJ: Rutgers University.

South African Literacy Students. (1985). *We came to town.* Johannesburg, South Africa: Ravan Press.

Tan, A. (1989). *The Joy Luck Club.* New York: Putnam.

Vasquez, E.P.M. (1986). *The story of Ana, La historia de Ana.* Pasadena, CA: Hope Publishing House. (P.O. Box 60008, Pasadena, CA 91106)

Vigil, E. (Ed.). (1987). *Woman of her word: Hispanic women write.* Houston: Arte Público Press.

Wolkstein, D. (Ed.). (1978). *The magic orange tree and other Haitian folktales.* New York: Schocken Books.

Women's kit. (1987). Toronto: Participatory Research Group/ICAE Women's Program.

Classroom Resources: Journals of Student Writings

Hear my soul's voice. (Available from Jefferson Park Writing Center, 6 Jefferson Park, Cambridge, MA 02140)

Mosaic. (Available from The After School Project, South Boston High School, 95 G St., South Boston, MA 02127)

Need I say more: A literary magazine of adult student writings. (Available from Adult Literacy Resource Institute, c/o Boston Business School, 989 Commonwealth Ave., Boston, MA 02215)

Voices: New writers for new readers. Invergarry Learning Centre, Surrey, British Columbia. (In the United States, available from Delta Systems Co., 570 Rock Road Dr., Unit H, Dundee, IL 60118-9922)

A writer's voice. (Available from 265 Gerrard Street East, Toronto, Ontario, Canada M5A 2G3)

Evaluation: References and Resources

Brindley, G. (1989). *Assessing achievement in the learner-centred curriculum.* Sydney, Australia: National Centre for English Language Teaching and Research, Macquarie University. (Distributed by Dominie Press)

Focus on Basics (1988). 2(1). (Special issue on assessment available from World Education, 210 Lincoln St., Boston, MA 02111)

Kucer, S.B. (n.d.). *Using informal evaluation to promote change in the literacy curriculum.* Unpublished manuscript. (Available from Dept. of Curriculum, Teaching, and Special Education, Graduate School of Education, Waite Phillips Hall, Rm. 1001E, University of Southern California, Los Angeles, CA 90089)

Lytle, S., & Wolfe, M. (1989). *Adult literacy education: Program evaluation and learner assessment.* Columbus, OH: ERIC Clearinghouse on Adult, Career and Vocational Education. (Ohio State University, 1900 Kenny Rd., Columbus, OH 43210-1090)

(To get information about an ad hoc seminar on appropriate literacy evaluation, contact Susan Harman, New York Public Interest Research Group, 9 Murray St., New York, NY 10007)

Journals about Literacy/ Adult Education

Connections: A journal of adult literacy. Adult Literacy Resource Institute, c/o Boston Business School, 989 Commonwealth Ave., Boston, MA 02215.

Convergence. International Council for Adult Education, 29 Prince Arthur Ave., Toronto, Ontario, Canada M5R 1B2.

Dialogue. (1982-1989). Center for Applied Linguistics, 1118 22nd St. NW, Washington, DC 20037. (Only back issues available)

Focus on basics. World Education, 210 Lincoln St., Boston, MA 02111.

The Ladder. Push Literacy Action Now. 1332 G St. SE, Washington, DC 20003.

Research and practice in adult literacy bulletin. RaPAL, Bolton Royd Centre, Manningham Lane, Bradford BD8 7BB, West Yorkshire, UK.

Voices rising: A bulletin about women and popular education. ICAE Women's Program. (See address below)

Addresses for Additional Resources

Dominie Press, Inc.
11568 Sorrento Valley Rd. #12
San Diego, CA 92121

Lutheran Settlement House
1340 Frankford Ave.
Philadelphia, PA 19125

National Clearinghouse on Literacy Education for Limited-English Proficient Adults and Out of School Youth (NCLE)
1118 22nd St. NW
Washington, DC 20037

Ontario Ministry of Citizenship
77 Bloor St. West, 5th Fl.
Toronto, Ontario M7A 2R9
Canada

The Oral History Center
186 1/2 Hampshire St.
Cambridge, MA 02139

For Participatory Research Group (PRG) publications, contact:
Popular Education Research Group
606 Shaw St.
Toronto, Ontario M6G 3L6
Canada

or:
PRG/ICAE Women's Program
c/o ICAE Secretariat
720 Bathurst St., Suite 500
Toronto, Ontario M5S 2R4
Canada

World Education
210 Lincoln St.
Boston, MA 02111